PRAISE
FEARLESS
SCHOOLS

"In this illuminating book, Doug Reeves addresses a critical issue in education: trust. Marshaling research from across many fields, he forcefully demonstrates that trust is the 'coin of the realm' that makes learning possible, not only for students but for teachers, administrators, and trustees as well. Trust removes fear and turns missteps and mistakes into opportunities for growth. This is a book to be both devoured and savored." —David Chojnacki, Executive Director Emeritus, Near East South Asia Association of Schools

"No one cuts to the heart of an issue like Doug Reeves. If you want to know how to build trust and preserve it over the long haul, this is the book for you. We see the complete range of circumstances and the specifics of how trusted leaders act in dealing with innovation, commitments, decision-making, and resistance. Also included are the mistakes and myths that can sabotage a well-intentioned culture builder. Then the theme of trust and learning from mistakes is carried into two other vital areas: personal resilience and wise classroom practice. The final touch is integrating these strategies with our best knowledge for leading change and systems thinking. The prose is, in turn, graceful and pointed, funny and poignant. *Fearless Schools* is filled with wisdom and stories that keep us on the reading and learning journey like a novel you can't put down." —Jon Saphier, CEO, Research for Better Teaching

"The students, teachers, and leaders who left us prior to the pandemic are not the same people who have returned to our schools. Many have been changed by the pain of the pandemic and the trauma that our school communities have endured. We will not overcome and achieve without building a foundation of trust, strong relationships, and the cultivation of fearless organizations. In *Fearless Schools: Building Trust and Resilience for Learning, Teaching, and Leading*, Dr. Doug Reeves shares a brilliant framework that places relationships and connections at the heart of this work. It is an exceptional guide for healing and growth in education." —Dr. Rosa Perez-Isiah, Author: *Beyond Conversations About Race*

FEARLESS
SCHOOLS

BUILDING **TRUST** AND **RESILIENCE** FOR **LEARNING**, **TEACHING**, AND **LEADING**

DOUGLAS REEVES

Creative Leadership Press
Boston, Massachusetts

Paperback ISBN 978-1-954744-20-2
Hardcover ISBN 978-1-954744-21-9
eBook ISBN 978-1-954744-22-6

Library of Congress Control Number 2021908028

Distributed by Epigraph Books, Rhinebeck, New York

Book and cover design by Colin Rolfe
Front cover background photo by Susan Gold

Creative Leadership Press
100 Beacon Street
Boston, MA 02116
(617) 952-8542
service@creativeleadership.net

For the Reverend Doctor Robert Allan Hill,
a fearless leader and faithful friend.

ACKNOWLEGMENTS

Footnotes and reference lists are wholly inadequate to describe the debt of authors to their sources. Harvard Professor Amy Edmondson is a pioneer in global research on psychological safety. She shares her research and work with many publications, including her extraordinary book, *The Fearless Organization*. It should be required reading for leaders at every level. Dr. Carol Kauffman, founder of the Institute of Coaching, an affiliate of McLean Hospital and part of the Harvard Medical School, provides a rich international perspective on best (and worst) practices in leadership coaching. She brings scholarship and rigor to a field that often lacks both of those qualities. Dr. John Hattie is perhaps the most influential educational researcher on the planet and also, in his Kiwi vernacular, a fine mate. Kim Marshall's Marshall Memo provides an indispensable source of research from more research sources than most people could read in a lifetime.

My colleagues at Creative Leadership Solutions devote themselves to taking on the toughest educational challenges, and they do so with a wonderful combination of intensity, intellectual curiosity, and good humor. They take their work, but not themselves, seriously—I am lucky indeed to have them as colleagues and friends. They include Alan Crawford, Alexandra Guilamo, Ann McCarty Perez, Bill Sternberg, Brian McNulty,

Christine Smith, David Aguado, David Gleason, Emily Freeland, Gregory VanHorn, Jo Peters, Joshua Faden, Karen Power, Kate Anderson-Foley, Ken Williams, Lisa Almeida, Lauren Mahoney, Linda O'Konek, Majalise Tolan, Maryellen Hinken, Mike Wasta, Pam VanHorn, Pete Ondish, Stacy Scott, Tony Flach, and Washington Collado.

The production team for this book included Creative Leadership Solutions internal editor Allison Amy Wedell—with publisher Paul Cohen, book designer Colin Rolfe, and editor Dory Mayo of Epigraph Publishing Service—whose expert advice and thoughtful encouragement made the manuscript clearer and more effective than had it been left to my own devices.

Bob Hill, to whom this book is dedicated, shepherds his global flock through the darkest times of the pandemic and other calamities, global and personal. When the world is fearful, he is fearless. In our darkest hours, he encourages those in despair, gives hope to the hopeless, and always leaves us with the confidence of a brighter day ahead. Every week, he reminds his listeners in Marsh Chapel in Boston and around the world that our mission is not only half a world away, but also half a block away. He carries on the tradition of the Irish-American poet Finely Peter Dunne to comfort the afflicted and afflict the comfortable, reminding us that to whom much is given, much is required. Whether he is serving as a Boston University Dean; a professor preparing the next generation of religious and secular leaders; a prolific writer whose erudite words instruct the reader one moment, to be moved to tears in the next; a visitor to the sick, bereaved, and dying; or a faithful Methodist fighting for justice within his own denomination—Dean Hill is the person that his students aspire to be when they grow up. On top of all that, he is a true, courageous, and loyal friend.

DOUGLAS REEVES

Boston, Massachusetts

April 2021

CONTENTS

PREFACE

A S THIS BOOK GOES to press, the world is slowly emerging from the global pandemic of 2020–2021 and its attendant economic and educational calamities. The personal cost of this crisis to families is beyond estimation. In the United States alone, it exceeds 500,000 in lost lives—adding illness, family disruption, isolation, depression, and trauma to the incalculable toll. Elsewhere around the globe the cost in uncounted deaths may never be fully known. Clearly, the sacred responsibility of those who survive is to honor the lost with a new resolve for equity, decency, and fairness that is greater and stronger than ever before. The central challenge to every reader of this book, therefore, is whether we will return to business as usual, thinking, "Thank goodness that's over; now we can return to life as it was." Or will we make decisions—for ourselves, our loved ones, our students, and our communities—to treasure the value of lessons purchased at an unspeakable price and determine to open schools that are safer, better, and, in a word, *fearless*?

We need not wait for historians to debate the lessons of this global crisis. Every educator, leader, parent, grandparent, and student knows that the most important lesson of the pandemic is that relationships matter. That was true before the pandemic, and it is truer now more than ever. No amount of technological sophistication can replace the human need for three-dimensional relationships. To put a fine point on it, screens can't hug. We know that resilience and psychological safety, the essence of this book, stem not from computer-generated formulae but from the teachers, parents, and leaders who say with conviction, "I believe in you."

When the history books of 2050 are published, they will have only a few paragraphs about the pandemic of 2020–2021. But in the year 2050, the world will still be haunted by the students we failed to serve—those who dropped out because they were not lucky enough to be in a fearless school with fearless teachers and fearless leaders. These students who failed to receive essential support will, in 2050, continue to suffer the rages of poverty and unemployment. They will continue to make disproportionate use of the medical care and criminal justice systems, and their needs and the needs of their families will continue well into the second half of the 21st century. It doesn't have to be that way. *Fearless Schools* provides a blueprint for a better future. The choice is ours. The time to make that choice is now.

BEING FEARLESS IN A FEARFUL TIME

QUICK: WHICH HOSPITAL HAS higher rates of medical errors? The first is a low-trust environment characterized by hierarchy, in which the doctor is always the smartest person in the room and whose authority is unquestioned. The second is a high-trust environment, in which all medical staff, including nurses, lab technicians, and therapists are all empowered to challenge authority when they believe it is in the best interest of the patient. Which hospital reports more errors? You might be tempted, as I was, to say, "Of course, the high-trust environment has fewer errors." But you would be wrong. As Harvard Business School Professor Amy Edmondson (2018) has discovered in more than two decades of research on the subject, high-trust hospitals actually report more errors than their low-trust counterparts. This is true not because the high-trust hospitals make more errors but because their pervasive sense of psychological safety allows them to report more errors and learn from them. Low-trust hospitals make lots of mistakes as well, but the environment of distrust and fear makes it unlikely that these mistakes will be reported. Thus, it becomes impossible for the staff to learn from them. High-trust organizations are, in Edmondson's words, fearless, and I am indebted to her for inspiring the title of this book.

People in high-trust organizations are not necessarily smarter or better educated than people in low-trust organizations. However, people in high-trust organizations are persistently engaged in learning as individuals and teams throughout the entire organization. Every mistake is an opportunity not for humiliation but for analysis, reflection, and learning. In this regard, high-trust hospitals mirror the characteristics of high-trust classrooms, collaborative teacher teams, cabinet meetings, and governing-board deliberations.

Consider the opposite of this learning environment, the fearful school. When fear is the motivator, students are not motivated by learning but by avoiding punishment. Sometimes the punishment to be avoided is a low grade or a stern glance from the teacher or administrator. If we have learned anything in a century of research on grading, it is that grading as punishment is ineffective and counterproductive (Guskey, 2014). To put the inadequacy of fearful learning environments in even more stark perspective, consider the case of corporal punishment. To the national shame of the US, 19 states continue to permit teachers and administrators to hit students as punishment (Schott Foundation, 2019). More than 600 students, from preschool to high school, suffer corporal punishment in the US every day. This affects not only the students who are being beaten but also every student and faculty member in the school who witnesses this barbarity. If you want the very definition of the fearful school, look no further than an environment in which misbehavior is not corrected but punished with a board, whip, ruler, or hand of an adult. Those states that have prohibited corporal punishment should not be complacent. In my work in 50 states, I continue to witness the impulse to use suspensions, isolation, low grades, and failure as motivational techniques designed to improve student performance. Adults also operate in an environment of fear, where perverse evaluation systems are not designed to provide meaningful feedback to improve performance; rather, their design demonstrates that the educational system is failing (Ravitch, 2010). Indeed, whether the instrument of punishment is a ruler, board, pen, or typewriter—the impact is the same: Trust is displaced by fear.

In the chapters that follow, you will learn why trust is essential to learning, from the youngest primary school student to the most experienced teacher and administrator. You will learn how to build and maintain trust in your school, and how quickly trust can be destroyed. We will explore how fearless schools support the emotional and mental health of students by building resilience in students and staff members. Resilient people are not immune from mistakes, but they have the emotional and intellectual ability to recognize mistakes, accept feedback from others, and bounce back from those errors. Resilient people combine the best of babies and rocket scientists, as both of these seemingly disparate groups relentlessly explore, test hypotheses, make many mistakes, and learn from each one. We then turn our attention to the daily reality of fearless schools, considering the perspectives of students, faculties, and leaders.

Fear is nothing new to students. They fear disapproval of adults, exclusion by peers, and their own sense of doubt and unworthiness. Add to the normal fears of childhood and adolescence the impact of the global pandemic of 2020 and the economic insecurity that follows for years afterwards, the loss of loved ones, and a continuing sense of uncertainty about the future—and the pervasive sense of fear in schools is understandable. The purpose of this book is to help educators, school leaders, parents, and policymakers create fearless schools despite a fearful environment.

PART I:

THE TRUST
IMPERATIVE

E VERYTHING DEPENDS ON TRUST. Personal relationships, the global economy, and our ability to have a sense
of purpose and meaning in our lives—all depend upon the
fundamental trust equation that our actions, resources, and emotional energy have value (Frei & Moriss, 2020). While we do not
depend upon reciprocity for all of our work—the Newtonian dictum
that for every action there is an equal and opposite reaction—we
do expect that our investment of time, energy, resources, and emotions are not in vain, and this first section of the book explores that
necessity.

Chapter 1 considers the research on the trust advantage. We
will learn how trust not only improves the morale and confidence of students and staff members but also how high-trust
organizations have better performance on every measure. This is
a global phenomenon, with similar advantages to trust occurring
in a wide variety of cultures, languages, and nations. Chapter 2
provides practical guidelines for building trust. Schools and educational systems are hierarchical organizations with governing

boards, superintendents, principals, department chairs, and other levels of hierarchy. And hierarchies, no matter how benevolent the leader may be, are breeding grounds for mistrust. Thus, good intentions and personal trustworthiness are helpful but insufficient to build trust in schools and systems. Chapter 3 considers the maintenance of trust and how it requires a consistent effort and rhythm of promises made and promises kept. While leaders will be forgiven for many mistakes if they have credibility, none of their skills in analysis, communication, or planning will matter if they have failed to establish credibility (Kouzes & Posner, 2011). Chapter 4 considers how trust that may take years to build can be destroyed in a moment with exaggerated claims or falsehoods, or with a rash impulse toward punishment.

THE TRUST ADVANTAGE

In this chapter—
- Learning
- Morale
- Impact
- Innovation

FEARLESS ORGANIZATIONS ARE CHARACTERIZED by high levels of trust. In fields as diverse as manufacturing, medical care, software development, and education, fearless organizations have greater productivity and higher levels of employee engagement and innovation (Edmondson, 2018). Trust and psychological safety are better predictors of performance of teams than educational backgrounds and personality types, the criteria often used to select and promote employees. Indeed, the tight-lipped diplomacy that is often associated with an upward career trajectory reinforces the code of silence. That behavior is precisely the opposite of that needed in a psychologically safe environment. What may appear on the outside as diplomacy can be, in fact, a reflection of fear—fear of conflict and fear of error—and these fears undermine learning. In this chapter we will explore why trust is essential for learning at every level, from the individual student to the faculty, leadership team, and governing board. The fearless school has four clear advantages over schools where fear and silence are the rule of the day. These advantages include learning, morale, impact, and innovation.

LEARNING

A high-trust environment has clear advantages for student learning (Modono, 2017). This does not imply a climate of happy talk in which disagreements are avoided in the pursuit of a positive culture. Rather, respectful but difficult discussions are part of the environment, because divergent thinking and a consideration of alternative points of view are keys to learning for adults and students. Fearless learning requires a culture of curiosity in which the candid acknowledgment of what we don't know is not a mark of shame or ignorance but a reflection of the deep desire to learn. It's difficult to imagine Copernicus or Galileo wilting with fear in the face of a multiple-choice test about the cosmos. Our images of great explorers are those of insatiable curiosity, embracing the unknown not with certainty but with a quest for learning.

When viewed from an intellectual standpoint, curiosity is a valued trait; but we have several hundred years of negative stereotypes to overcome in order to make this trait a valuable part of education. The phrase "curiosity killed the cat" can be traced to a play by Ben Johnson in the 16th century (Literary Devices, n.d.), and through the ages the meaning has been consistent: Curiosity, especially about things that are not of immediate relevance to you, can be dangerous. Stay in your lane, be satisfied with your present state of knowledge, and don't ask unpleasant questions. As the parents of toddlers know, one of the first words our darlings learn, right after "No!" is "Why?" It's charming the first time, and perhaps the second. But after the 10th time, it becomes irksome, and the exasperated parent replies, in a tone that defies challenge, "Because I said so!" Thus do we extinguish curiosity before children first cross the threshold of the school-house door. Picasso said "Every child is an artist. The problem is how to remain an artist once we grow up" (Chase, 2014). So the reason that trust is vital to learning is that in order to learn, we must ask questions; we must try and fail. And in order to ask questions, try, and fail, we must have confidence that our curiosity won't kill us or, even worse, disappoint our parents.

MORALE

Morale is key to success in any organization and is strongly related to peak performance of employees and leaders. Morale is the result of leadership actions, not rhetoric: "You can't boss your way out of a morale problem" (Mallik et al., 2019). Leaders can neither demand trust nor beg for it; first, they must trust their colleagues and employees. Everyone brings to the workplace memories of every job, from the teenage summer job in which they were berated by a manager, to their previous position in which political gamesmanship was elevated over competence. In hierarchies—and schools and educational systems are hierarchical systems, notwithstanding any claims to democratic rules and commitments to consensus—leaders are separated from those on the front line. Every gap in communication is filled in with assumptions, and these assumptions are colored not just by the present work environment, but by previous ones. This is true of the adults in schools and most especially true of students. Leaders must actively show trust by asking open-ended questions, listening without judgment or debate, and expressing genuine curiosity through follow-up questions.

Leaders can also create a culture of trust in which morale is genuine and enduring by showing respect and allowing creativity to thrive (Schaefer, 2019). Creativity requires not merely the expression of brilliant ideas, but a seemingly endless cycle of trial, error, and disappointment. Creativity thrives not because of the presence of the mythical muse (Reeves & Reeves, 2016) but because people have the confidence to make mistakes and learn from them, trusting that their peers and bosses will forgive the mistakes that are inevitably made in the pursuit of learning.

IMPACT

In her research involving countries around the world with organizations with widely varying missions—including education, government, health care, and industry—Edmondson found that high levels of trust are associated with significant gains in problem-solving, teamwork, and employee satisfaction, all of which lead to a significantly positive impact on organizational performance (Edmondson, 2018). Moreover, high-trust organizations perform significantly better than their peers in employee satisfaction and a wide range of financial indicators (Covey & Conant, 2016).

It is not just organizational performance that is influenced by a high-trust environment. Individual performance is also strongly related to trust in leaders and organizations (Judeh, 2016). This is particularly important during periods of change (Ouslis, 2019). When employees only hear the announcements of changes without understanding the rationale behind these changes— emotional distance, distrust, and paralysis can follow. This is true not only of large-scale changes, such as reorganizations, but also of seemingly small changes, such as the relocation of desks or offices. Change is associated with fear, and fear breeds distrust.

INNOVATION

Oxford University researchers have concluded that trust and innovation are inseparable (M.-L. Marshall, 2018). Without trust, innovation is not possible. The granting of trust is a voluntary decision and cannot be compelled. It depends on four traits: competence, reliability, benevolence, and integrity. While each of these traits is not subject to specific quantification, people are acutely aware of their absence. The supremely competent person, for example, may be inconsistent, and therefore lack reliability. Or perhaps they have these traits but lack empathy, the key to benevolence. Even with these three traits, integrity remains the cornerstone of trust—for without it, trust is impossible, and without trust, innovation is an illusion. Innovation requires risk, and people will never take risks in an environment that lacks trust.

In this chapter we have considered the effect of trust on learning and morale, and its impact on ingenuity and productivity. When leaders create and maintain a culture of trust, from the team to the entire organization, both individual and group learning is in overdrive. Because high-trust groups can talk about their mistakes, they can learn from them and they can help new team members understand the necessity of trust and open discussion of both successes and failures. High-trust organizations also create a virtuous cycle, in which trust leads to better morale—and high levels of morale, in turn, lead to greater degrees of trust. The impact of trust is dramatic, not only in terms of employee satisfaction but also with regard to innovation, creativity, and financial performance. When it comes to organizational health, it all starts and ends with trust.

It is, however, much easier to talk about the virtues of trust than the mechanics of building trust. This requires counterintuitive actions by leaders who, on the one hand, must instill confidence throughout the organization in the competence of the leadership team and, on the other hand, must be sufficiently vulnerable to acknowledge mistakes and seek help from colleagues at every level. Modern organizations are often overwhelmed with data, but the same information can be used either as a weapon to humiliate employees and instill fear throughout the organization, or to seek insights. And, as we will see in the next chapter, the appropriate use of data as a tool of inquiry is inextricably linked to a culture of responsibility. Fearless schools and fearless educational systems are not built on the illusion of perfection but on the firm foundation of facts. Fearless leaders do not fill in gaps of knowledge or silence of team members with worst-case scenarios or assumptions, nor do they assume that all is well without the data to support these assumptions. They know that trust requires the embrace of reality in an environment of mutual respect and personal reasonability.

DISCUSSION QUESTIONS

1. Think of a teacher or school administrator in whom you placed complete trust. Reflect on a situation in which you made a mistake. Please describe what happened, what the mistake was, and how the teacher or administrator reacted to it. How does this experience inform your interactions with students and colleagues today?

2. What was the hardest thing you ever learned, inside or

outside of school? What made it so difficult? How did you overcome the difficulties in learning?

3. Think of an instance in which your trust was misplaced—that is, you trusted an individual or organization, and you later learned that this individual or organization was not trustworthy. How did this breach of trust influence your interactions with that individual or organization?

4. Reflecting on the breach of trust in the previous question, consider the months and years that followed. Did your reactions change over time, or were they permanent? Is there anything that this individual or institution could do to regain your trust?

5. Think of a time when you or your team developed something especially creative. What were the conditions that supported your creativity? Please describe the relationships among your team and relationships with your supervisors and evaluators.

CHAPTER 2.

BUILDING TRUST

In this chapter—

- The Neuroscience of Trust
- How Leaders Build Trust
- Data Analysis: From the Witch Hunt to the Treasure Hunt
- How Colleagues Build Trust
- Personal Responsibility and Trust

T HIS CHAPTER BEGINS WITH trust not just as an emotional factor in the relationships among people in organizations but with the neuroscience of trust. Profoundly important physiological and chemical changes in the human body are associated with high and low levels of trust. Building trust, we will learn, is not about rhetoric or posters on the wall but about the daily actions, habits, and decisions that leaders make. Their decisiveness can help to build trust, as can their reluctance to make hasty decisions when more inclusion, more information, and more deliberation is necessary. While many organizations pride themselves on data-driven decisions, data can be used wisely to understand conflicting information and nuance, or data can be weaponized to cast blame or claim certainty in an uncertain reality. Trust is not the sole responsibility of the leader; it is a reflection of collegial interactions.

One of the best descriptions of the essential nature of trust was summarized by Engelman and colleagues:

> Trust pervades almost every aspect of human social life. It plays a decisive role in families, organizations, markets, and the political sphere. Without trust, families fall apart, organizations are inefficient, market transactions are costly, and political leaders lack public support. Research in behavioral economics and neuroeconomics has begun to elucidate the determinants and neural correlates of trust. (Engleman et al., 2019).

THE NEUROSCIENCE OF TRUST

More than a decade of research (Zak, 2017) shows that trust is not merely a psychological issue, but a physiological one as well. Researchers can monitor levels of oxytocin, a powerful hormone that influences behavior and relationships, and how oxytocin measurements change depending on how individuals grant trust and receive trust from others. Oxytocin is as close as we have to a naturally occurring miracle drug. People with higher levels of this hormone, prompted by increased levels of trust, have greater productivity, fewer sick days, greater engagement at work, greater satisfaction in their personal lives, and less burnout.

Analysis of brain scans of experimental participants revealed that fear reduced trust and risk-taking, both essential qualities for creativity, innovation, and organizational success. Moreover, the fear induced in these experiments directly affected the amygdala, the part of the brain associated with the fight, flight, or freeze response (Engleman et al., 2019). It is a short trip—from the fear of ancient predators and distrust of the member of the tribe who fails to share the spoils of the hunt—to the conference room in which the boss rules by fear and colleagues fail to share credit. Our reactions to these situations are not entirely rational and controllable; rather, they surge from deep within our brain. While some people are capable of camouflaging fear, no one is capable of avoiding it.

HOW LEADERS BUILD TRUST

In order to build trust and the positive neurological benefits associated with it, several specific strategies are available to leaders and educators. First, we must recognize excellence. A Bain & Company study of organizations around the world (Mankins & Garton, 2017) concluded that one of the best employee benefits for A+ players is the opportunity to work with other A+ players, and one of the most demotivating leadership practices is the toleration of mediocrity. Recognition need not always be in the form of bonuses and promotions but can also come in the form of feedback that is accurate, sincere, and immediate.

Challenging, but achievable, tasks boost not only oxytocin but also adrenocorticotropin, another chemical linked to focus, concentration, and energy. These chemical reactions happen when both great victories and incremental progress are achieved. Even on long-term challenges, personal and team engagement depends upon the principle of daily progress, the small wins that are the building blocks of great achievements (Hansen et al., 2018). Another important strategy to enhance the motivation of colleagues is professional discretion and independence. This is not a prescription for anarchy; rather, it is the path toward the agency and self-determination that people crave. One study (Feintzeig,

2014) suggested that people would give up a 20 percent raise in order to secure more autonomy on the job. This is consistent with the findings in schools by University of Pennsylvania researcher Richard Ingersoll, who has studied teacher turnover for three decades. He reports that it is not low salaries alone that drive teachers out of the profession, but a lack of autonomy and inadequate working conditions (Phillips, 2015).

These prescriptions for building trust are counterintuitive for senior leaders who operate in an environment with a limited tolerance for failure. They cling to a command-and-control style of leadership in which information is held closely and procedures on everything from hallway passes to curriculum to assessments are regulated in exacting detail. The minute-to-minute message to subordinates is that they may think they are professionals, but we trust them less than manual laborers. It is not that we are without the research and knowledge of how to build trust but that we lack the courage to trust our colleagues and subordinates.

DATA ANALYSIS: FROM THE WITCH HUNT TO THE TREASURE HUNT

At the heart of the culture of fearless schools is the way in which leaders display and discuss data on student performance. Two starkly different approaches characterize leadership and data analysis. While the technology, graphs, and data displays may be identical, the leadership lens through which data are examined and the consequent learning from those analyses could not be more different. The fearful leader displays the data in the unfortunately named "war room," a commonly used label in many schools I have visited. It's not entirely clear who the enemy is, but teachers fear that they might be on the wrong side of this particular battle. There are three ways in which leaders can display data: humiliation, distortion, and learning.

Humiliation is commonly associated with data displays. Results such as test scores, attendance, and discipline purport to show the successes of some teachers and schools and the failures of others. Any attempt to explain low performance is regarded as an excuse, not analysis. Attendance is down? Don't tell me about poor transportation options or the need for some teenagers to care for younger siblings, and don't tell me about absent parents. What are you going to do about it? In the midst of the COVID-19 pandemic, when schools around the world were closed, I asked the administration in one high-poverty school, where more than 90 percent of the students qualified for free or reduced-price lunch, why some students were failing to log in to the online learning that the school had arranged. "Because they are lazy," came the immediate response. While the school had provided laptop computers for every student and made great efforts to provide internet connectivity for homes throughout the community, educational leaders had not taken into account what was happening inside the home. In one case, the mother had been called to duty with the National Guard, leaving the father with five children fighting over one computer while he worked from home. In other cases, teenage students were taking on manual-labor day jobs to help their single parent, who had been laid off, put food on the table. The central problem with most data analysis is that it assumes a single cause for a single effect. If the result we seek is better attendance, either physically or virtually, and the only cause we consider is the ineptitude of administrators and teachers or the laziness of students, then other vitally important causes are ignored. This sort of data analysis by humiliation conveys a sense of futility and helplessness that reinforces fear.

The second approach to analysis is data distortion. Rather than risk humiliation, administrators and teachers can simply distort the data. The most common distortion is to homogenize the data, burying insights under a larger pile of numbers so that school and district averages are displayed. This prevents any meaningful insights about the underlying causes of differences in results. These differences might be associated with the professional practices that vary from one school to another and one classroom to another, and might be related to a host of other causes. That perspective is the essence of systems thinking, a subject we will take up in Chapter 11. In a fearless school, teachers can observe differences and ask, "Your students did so well on that test of fractions and decimals. Please tell me more about what you did to make that happen." In the fearful school, no such insights are possible because there are no displays that separate one classroom from another. In the fearful district, data are not compared among schools; rather, only district averages are displayed, thus preventing meaningful insights about the leadership practices of individual schools. To be sure, there are many factors that influence achievement and attendance beyond the practices of teachers and leaders, and these factors can also be fruitful topics of conversation. "We both had similar percentages of special education students, ESL students, and students in poverty, but your data suggest that you had significantly better attendance and achievement. Please tell me more about that." This spirit of inquiry is at the heart of how fearless schools conduct data analysis. In the fearful school, inquiry is not possible because the fear surrounding the presentation of school and district averages renders deep understanding impossible.

A more pernicious distortion of data occurs not through homogenization but through deceit. You want better discipline data? No problem, we just won't report student misbehavior.

You want better test scores? No problem, we can fix that, as did a dozen administrators and teachers in Atlanta, 11 of whom were convicted of felonies and sentenced to lengthy prison terms (Blinder, 2015). You want better attendance; we can fix that too. In one urban district I observed, the calculation of daily attendance was the responsibility of each school's administrative assistant, and each one had strikingly different methods of calculating and reporting it. As quality-guru W. Edwards Deming said, every system is perfectly designed to get the results it gets (MacDevey, 2018). Consider the case of high school graduation. The Every Student Succeeds Act (ESSA), passed in 2016, required states to report high school graduation rates as part of their accountability measurements. Within a very short period of time, high schools around the nation reported giant leaps in graduation rates. Some of these gains were due to exceptional teaching, focus, and leadership. But other gains were illusory. I witnessed one student achieve a full semester's worth of credit by participating in an online course for less than three hours. His teachers explained to me that this was typical—if high school graduation is what is expected, then they could produce it through the magic of courses that granted credit without the burdensome tasks of teaching and learning.

The final approach to data analysis is the unpopular but essential path of learning. This requires the leadership courage to elevate facts over fantasy and reality over wishful thinking. It also requires a spirit of resilience and confidence in which teachers and administrators face unpleasant data on student performance with the belief that they are trusted to use the data in a constructive manner and that, in turn, they trust their leaders not to use the data to harm them professionally or hurt them personally. This does not mean that we ignore data on poor performance but that we use the data constructively. One way in which leaders can express this approach is the following: No one will be blamed for the data. Our accountability is not about the data; rather, it is about how we respond to the data. Action and constructive response are required, and indifference is not acceptable.

HOW COLLEAGUES BUILD TRUST

Building trust is difficult under the best of circumstances, such as when we share coffee, face-to-face meetings, and social gatherings. But building and maintaining trust is particularly challenging without these interpersonal connections. Whether your colleagues are in a different building, school, or continent, there are complexities of building trust in organizations large and small. We cannot assume, however, that physical presence is equivalent to mental and emotional presence. So many meetings include participants whose attention is so fragmented that sitting across the table from someone may be little different in terms of emotional engagement than participating in a video conference half a world away (Rogelberg, 2019). This is particularly true when virtual meetings have become the norm, but we dare not delude ourselves into thinking that two-dimensional communication is a substitute for the nuances of body language, eye movement, and subtle gestures that are only apparent in live interactions.

Researchers have identified two types of trust among colleagues: swift trust and passable trust (Neeley, 2018). Swift trust is a function of direct interaction. It is the result of an immediate decision, informed by physical, facial, and behavioral signals. Sometimes swift trust is the default. When colleagues are thrown into a room together, they know that they had better get along and trust one another, or they are going to have a very unpleasant job experience. Swift trust is also an artifact of crisis situations, such as teams in emergency rooms, law enforcement response teams, or air crews who must work together to respond to in-flight emergencies. Swift trust can be aided or undermined based on how new members are introduced to the team. "Janice is new and will be joining us today," is tepid compared to "We are so lucky to have Janis joining the team, as her experience in assessment and emotional resilience of adolescents will be especially valuable for our department and our students. I've spoken with her former colleagues, who said that she is not only a great colleague because of her expertise but also someone whom we can trust to both support and challenge our thinking."

Passable trust is more subtle than swift trust, as it depends upon some inquiry and inference by the person granting the trust. We might notice, for example, that a colleague has been willing to share expertise and resources on social media and internal organizational websites. Research at the University of Pennsylvania (Grant, 2013) suggests that sharing requires a delicate balance. The "givers" in Grant's terminology are not pushovers or doormats, but they build reputations for helping colleagues and, in particular, for helping colleagues who are lateral or junior to them in the organization. That is, the faculty department head who is always willing to offer help to administrators at the building and central office levels but has little time for new teaching colleagues, is not a giver. But the person building a network based on passable trust is helping people she may not even know. Her expertise is designed to help the entire school and world of education, whether or not there is reciprocity for her efforts. Although passable trust can be more ambiguous and difficult to establish than swift trust, it tends to be more permanent. Trust that is swiftly established can also evaporate swiftly.

Regardless of the manner in which trust is generated, it is essential. Trust cannot be forced on colleagues, but it can be nurtured with a combination of intentional listening, clearly evident respect, and an ethic of shared credit. Most of all, trust among colleagues is exemplified by the culture of learning that happens when we not only celebrate success but also discuss mistakes and the learning that can, in a high-trust environment, follow.

PERSONAL RESPONSIBILITY AND TRUST

In fearless schools, students and adults display personal responsibility. They take pride in their accomplishments and take responsibility for their inevitable mistakes. The culture of responsibility is the opposite of a culture of blame because, long before anyone else can point an accusatory finger at someone responsible for an error, they hear, "I own this, and I'm going to learn from it." One of the characteristics of personal responsibility that creates a trusting and fearless environment is the ability to set boundaries and respect the boundaries of others. High-performing colleagues are reluctant to decline a request to serve on a committee or task force. They are known as "fixers" because they are trusted to get things done (Wiseman, 2010).

The problem with fixers is that they are enmeshed in an unwinnable game of Whac-A-Mole: Every time they fix one problem, another one pops up. Because they are so fixated on solving problems, they never achieve the status of a "multiplier," the leader who empowers colleagues to also diagnose, fix, and most importantly, prevent problems. I have seen school leaders who are so proud of their role as fixers that they never fulfill their primary role as an instructional leader. They are, and I am not exaggerating, working on flat tires on the school bus, collecting trash in the cafeteria, and going to meetings in the central office two or more days a week. In their school office, they are answering an endless torrent of emails, texts, and Twitter posts, explaining to me that if they fail to respond immediately, they will disappoint their supervisors, parents, board members, and community stakeholders. This creates the illusion of productivity and burns the leaders to a cinder but all the while fails to help the students and faculty fulfill their primary obligations of teaching and learning.

By contrast, the leaders who are multipliers are able to maintain profound levels of trust and personal responsibility while setting boundaries that allow them to focus on their highest priorities. For example, they maintain their obligations to visit classrooms and be with students and teachers by being fully present with them. During these visits, their administrative assistant explains to callers and drop-in visitors that "she has a commitment." This language is important because not everyone—especially those who demand to speak with the principal or superintendent immediately—regards classroom visits as a priority. This language of commitment is useful not only for classroom visits but also for project work-time, solitude and reflection, and observation of collaborative teacher teams. In order to be fully present, these leaders use the "do not disturb" function on their phones, receiving only calls and texts that are genuine emergencies. While they are focused on their commitments, they are not sending or receiving emails or are otherwise distracted. Instead, they are fully engaged with the students and colleagues they serve. They know the folly of multitasking and the devastating toll this common practice takes on engagement, productivity, and relationships (MacKay, 2019). Rather than engaging in the futile attempt to fix every problem, they routinely empower others by refusing to come to the rescue. As seductive as being the reliable hero in every situation may be, these leaders know that the health of the school and the entire system depends not on heroes but on teams of people—students and adults—who collaborate to make the system work. Movies about educational heroes create the illusion of inspiration, but they do not represent sustainable models of success.

As the myths of ancient times instruct us, every hero has a fatal flaw. The dangers of heroic myths are equally relevant in the 21st century. I see it every day in emails sent by teachers and educational leaders at midnight and five in the morning. They sacrifice everything, including family relationships and their own health, in pursuit of the unattainable status of perpetual hero. Moreover, as there is no room for more than one hero in the drama, these heroes persist until they can no longer carry on, leaving the field of battle—educational, rhetorical, and physical—to the next hero. A sustainable system of leadership in a fearless school does not depend upon the dominance of the hero who singlehandedly saves the day. Fearlessness, in brief, is not about individual heroes, but about cultures in which thoughtful questions are more important than rhetorical certitude and brave-sounding boasts. Personal responsibility is not about the exceptional practices of a single person, but about the culture in which everyone shares responsibility, credit, and learning.

In this chapter we considered the neuroscience of trust, revealing that trust—or lack of trust—is not always a rational decision but can be influenced by reactions deep within our brain that are related to fear and confidence. The central message of neuroscience in this context is that fear is the thief of trust. Leaders build trust not with orations and slogans but with their personal example. They persistently replace the illusion of perfection with appropriate vulnerability, accepting criticism, asking for help, and admitting mistakes. While rational decision-making depends upon data, information can be used to threaten, intimidate, and embarrass our colleagues, or it can be used to seek out best practices and successes. In brief, effective data analysis is not weaponized as a destructive and threatening witch hunt; rather, it is an energizing and engaging treasure hunt. Moreover, as important as the quantitative data may be, there is always a qualitative lens through which we can better understand the data. There is, in brief, a story behind the numbers. Colleagues can build trust based on quick judgments, typically associated with face-to-face contact and first impressions. But passable trust can be more enduring and have greater systemwide impact. Finally, trust is directly related to the ability of leaders and team members to display personal responsibility. A culture of blame undermines trust, whereas a culture of personal responsibility encourages open communication and learning. In the next chapter we will explore how organizations maintain trust. The credibility of leaders and the organizations they serve is based on the rhythm of promises made and promises kept. Listening—especially deep listening without interruption—is an astoundingly difficult skill. Highly skilled professionals are often much more skilled at providing answers than they are at asking question and then, with exquisite patience, listening for the alternative answers.

DISCUSSION QUESTIONS

1. Research suggests that high levels of trust are related to powerful chemical reactions in the body. Think of times when you experienced such a "natural high" in which you felt a sense of empowerment and joy. Please describe one of these experiences in detail.

2. Think of a time, either during your professional career or in volunteer activities or before you entered the workforce, in which you were challenged to take on an especially difficult task that you ultimately accomplished. Please describe the task and the circumstances under which you took on this challenge. How did your leader convey to you that you were

the right person for this task? What feedback during your work on this task did you receive? What was your reward at the completion of the task?

3. Think of a time, either as a professional or a student, when data were weaponized—that is, the numbers were used to threaten, intimidate, and bully you and your colleagues. Recall, in as vivid detail as possible, what the numbers were and your feelings about those numbers. Exactly what were you supposed to do in response to the numbers? What was the end result? What happened months or years later as a result of this intimidating presentation of data?

4. Think of a time, either as a professional or as a student, when data were presented in a constructive manner. Recall, in as vivid detail as possible, what the numbers were and your feelings about those numbers. Exactly what were you supposed to do in response to the numbers? What was the end result? What happened months or years later as a result of this constructive presentation of data?

5. Think of examples of "swift trust" that was granted instantly and "passable" trust that was built over time. In your own experience in your professional life and outside of your work life, when have you given to another person or institution swift and passable trust? What differences did you notice over time?

6. Consider the contrast between "fixers" and "multipliers" in your own experience. When have you been a fixer, and what was the result? When were you a multiplier, and what was the result? Looking ahead, are there situations in which you might be tempted to be a fixer, but you can instead choose to be a multiplier?

CHAPTER 3

MAINTAINING TRUST

In this chapter—

- Promises Made, Promises Kept
- The Art and Science of Listening
- The Case for Candor
- Trust Through Disagreements
- The Challenges and Opportunities of Hierarchy

TRUST IS THE FOUNDATION of fearless schools, and the foundation of trust is leadership credibility. Maintaining trust and credibility requires consistent vigilance. Whether you are leading a single school or a complex educational system, it is important to remember that you are not driving a luxury car that needs maintenance only once every 3,000 miles. Perhaps a better metaphor is that leading a fleet of jumbo jets, you are responsible for thousands of lives. Pilots and flight engineers monitor the safety and performance of the aircraft every moment of the flight. Between each flight, ground technicians meticulously review every surface of the aircraft, inside and out, to assure continued safe flights. During turbulence, delays, or emergencies, the best pilots and flight crews communicate consistently with every passenger—offering calm, clear, and accurate information. If passengers need to brace for a hard landing, leaders do not equivocate but instruct the passengers to take positions that will best assure their safety. When all goes well, the captain shares credit with the crew and never assumes that a single person saved the day. Yet no matter how skilled the leader, hierarchical organizations, from the crew of an aircraft to the staff of a school or educational system, can be cauldrons of mistrust. Indeed, mistrust and the feeling that it was unsafe to discuss potential dangers have been at the heart of some of the world's worst aviation disasters. Surprisingly, however, hierarchy can be strongly related to trust when well executed. This explains why, when researchers asked people, "Who do you trust most," it was not surprising that politicians and business leaders scored fairly low. The highest trust? A group of people who must operate with hierarchy every day: school principals (Snow, 2020). As this chapter will show, it is difficult enough to establish trust. It is even harder to maintain it.

PROMISES MADE, PROMISES KEPT

One of the most robust research findings in the field of leadership trust is the impact of credibility (Kouzes & Posner, 2011). When it is established, it is an organization's most valuable asset. Leaders will be forgiven for errors in analysis, communication, and political judgment—as long as they maintain credibility with stakeholders. But no matter how skillful they are in data analysis, communication, and political judgment, those attributes are irrelevant if the leaders lack credibility. Even new employees with limited experience can establish credibility with colleagues and managers by leveraging their skills, building relationships, and most of all, keeping their promises (Wolinsky & Newfield, 2017).

There is a now-ancient term in computer software design called WYSIWYG, pronounced "whizzy wig." It stands for "what you see is what you get," and that is the key not only to intuitive computer interfaces but also to credibility throughout an organization. In the most effective organizations I have studied, there is a steady rhythm of promises made and promises kept:

- "At our last meeting, I promised that I would bring you the data on the relationship between student performance on our reading assessments and student performance in math, science, and social studies. Here is the information I promised."
- "At our last Professional Learning Community collaborative team meeting, we agreed that each of us would bring to this meeting two examples of student writing. Let's take a look."
- "At our last meeting, I promised I would find out the stipends of coaches for other schools in our area, and I wanted to let you know that I don't have that data yet, but I intend to keep that promise to you by next meeting. Please be patient with me. I just wanted to keep you posted on that promise and every promise that I make to you."

This litany of promises made and promises kept is an ideal way to start every meeting, from teams of teachers to meetings of departments, faculty, cabinets, and governing boards. As soon as the Pledge of Allegiance and other opening ceremonies are completed, a ritual of promises made and promises kept makes the point that these levels of individual and organizational integrity are right up there with the Pledge when it comes to upholding the values and principles of the school and district.

THE ART AND SCIENCE OF LISTENING

Too many leaders think that the art of leadership is all about talking—the clever remark, the eloquent speech, the inspiring oration. They are wrong. The consistent communication attribute that we seek in leaders is not talking, but listening (Itzchakov & Krueger, 2018). Unfortunately, many leaders who have excellent organizational and management skills are poor listeners, and this undermines their trust and credibility with peers and subordinates. The benefits of effective listening are overwhelming. They include helping the listener think more critically and consider multiple points of view, and giving the person being listened to a sense of respect and empowerment as well as lower levels of stress and anxiety. In both emotional and intellectual terms, therefore, listening is a powerful leadership practice.

If the evidence is so clear that listening works well, why do so many people fail at this critical skill in their personal and work relationships? First, listening cedes power and momentum to the person talking. It is very hard to listen to someone talk in the best of circumstances, especially when some of the things they are saying are, at least to the listener's view, just plain wrong. Moreover, listening is exhausting. It takes time and emotional energy, and it is difficult to conceal the fact that we would rather be doing many other things than listening. Perhaps the most difficult part of listening is the fear that we might be wrong and would therefore have to change our own points of view, opinions, and decisions. I cannot count the number of times I have heard educational leaders tell me that they were hired to be a change agent, and that they soon discovered that they were expected to change everything except the faculty, the views of the governing board, and a century or two or past practices. They might have asked, before a contract was signed, "Precisely what are you willing to change?" and listen without interruption to the awkward silence that follows such a question.

THE CASE FOR CANDOR

Almost everyone agrees that candor, at least as a matter of philosophy, is a good thing. Who could possibly be in favor of the opposite of candor? Who favors deceit, dissembling, and dishonesty? It turns out that many people do. We prefer happy talk to honest bad news. Early in my career as a leader, a colleague asked if I would prefer a sincere bad attitude or an insincere good attitude, and I responded definitively that I preferred the latter option. I feared conflict, being wrong, and personal challenges. I was lucky enough to have colleagues who pushed back on my presumption, and I learned great lessons about leadership as a result.

The alternatives to candor can seem congenial, but they are deadly to organizational trust and culture, as Kim Scott writes in her book *Radical Candor: Be a Kick-Ass Boss Without Losing Your Humanity*. Consider a two-by-two matrix in which care about people is placed on the vertical axis and commitment to performance reflected in direct challenges where appropriate is placed on the horizontal axis (Scott, 2017). The upper right-hand corner, at the intersection of high levels of care about the individual and high commitment to performance, is what Scott describes as compassionate candor. The lower right-hand column, the intersection of low personal care and high commitment to performance, is what Scott describes as obnoxious aggression. This is the quadrant most employees associate with conversations that begin with, "I want to give you some feedback" or "Let me coach you on this." The implication, before the conversation starts, is the employee is wrong and the boss is the exclusive possessor of knowledge.

While no one appreciates obnoxious aggression, kindness without a commitment to performance is also deadly. In the upper left-hand quadrant, where personal care is high and commitment to performance is low, Scott describes ruinous empathy. This starts in the early years of school when students are reluctant to give an honest criticism of one another's work, and continues in the educational careers of teachers and administrators who receive years of good or even very good evaluations, when their deficiencies are clear to everyone, including the person awarding these inaccurate evaluations. I often hear administrators and politicians blame the ills of public education on unions, especially the tenure rules. "You just can't fire an incompetent teacher," they complain. Yet often, when I dig into these cases I find that years, sometimes decades, have passed in which not a single administrator had the courage to give honest feedback on the incompetence of the employee and offer very specific coaching for improvement. Behind most of these teachers who are difficult to fire stands an evaluator unequal to the task.

The lower left-hand quadrant, with low personal care and low levels of performance commitment, Scott describes as manipulative insincerity. Every great teacher I know craves feedback, not just in terms of formal evaluations but in the application of new technology, strategies to engage students, and ideas to make learning relevant to the worlds of students. The greatest influence on student achievement is teacher quality, and the greatest threat to teacher quality is not the failure to fire poor teachers but the hemorrhage of good and great teachers from the profession. The research is clear that while money is important for educators, you can't sustain six-figure debt on a five-figure income; the over-whelming reason that teachers leave the classroom is not finan-cial but professional (D. Reeves, 2018). Poor working conditions and, above all, a lack of respect not only drives teachers out of the classroom but also prevents the most promising new teaching candidates from entering the profession.

Times of crisis and stress are particular threats to candor. There is a wide chasm between our instinctive impulses and the need for building a trusting environment through candor (Kerrissey & Edmondson, 2020). For example, our instinct in the face of bad news may be to wait for additional information. After all, perhaps there is light at the end of the tunnel. But as one wag put it, "It's always darkest just before it goes pitch black." A better response in the face of difficult information is to share it accurately and calmly but with a sense of urgency. Our instinct may be to downplay the bad, but fearless leaders communicate with transparency. The instinct of the fearful leader is to take pains to explain and justify previous decisions, while the fearless leader acknowledges mistakes, helps people learn from them, and moves ahead to apply that learning to future decisions. While fearful leaders insist on staying the course as the Titanic plunges into the iceberg and to the bottom of the ocean, fearless lead-ers are engaged in constant updating and course corrections. Leaders are best served when they receive input from a variety of experts, even when those experts disagree.

TRUST THROUGH DISAGREEMENTS

Diversity of opinion is not only essential for improved leader-ship decision-making but also can save lives. The most dramatic example of the impact of suppressed disagreement comes from studies of aviation disasters. While air travel remains the safest form of transportation—far safer than automobile travel—it is precisely this safety record that makes disasters headline news. In a review of some of the worst accidents in airline history (Barron, n.d.), there was a strikingly common cause. It was not mechanical failure or bad weather. Rather, the consistent cause that led to thousands of passenger deaths was miscommunication or, more likely, no communication among the cockpit crew and air traffic controllers. Airline captains achieved their lofty status by a combination of professional competence and a commanding presence. People trust them and are willing to follow them, especially when conditions are difficult. However, there can be a thin line between respect and reverence that suppresses essential information. In 2020, it is not unusual to see the entire crew, including cockpit crew and flight attendants, gathered for a briefing and introducing themselves to one another by first names. I've been able to observe some of these briefings, and they always end the same way. In so many words, the pilot says, "If anyone—any one of you—notices something that you find unusual or unacceptable, I need you to tell me about it right away." Failure to communicate on this timely and candid level prevented copilots from handling navigation errors, low fuel levels, and the presence of other aircraft. Incredibly, some of these accidents were caused by the pilot taking off from the wrong runway. One of the most basic pieces of equipment still used by pilots is the old-fashioned compass. If I am to take off on runway 36, then the compass should read 360, or due north. If I am to take off on runway 27, then the compass would read 270, or due west. Any deviation from this check can lead, and has led, to disaster.

Fearless pilots do not suppress unpleasant news but react to it decisively with genuine curiosity and inquiry. Similarly, fearless educational leaders do not shy away from difficult news. While test scores alone are never a complete reflection of student performance, leaders know that when only a fraction of students are reading proficiently, it is like a critical fuel shortage on a jumbo jet. If you don't fix that, every other system will fail. Deficits in literacy affect not only every other class in school but also have long-term influences on the prospects of the student graduating from high school and taking advantage of opportunities in the workplace or postsecondary education.

The conditions of meetings can obscure effective communication as much as the culture of hierarchy does. In the context of in-flight communication, the following causes were identified as leading to fatal miscommunication (Barron, n.d.). See if any of these are similar to your most recent meetings:

- noise
- multiple communications happening at once
- fatigue, stress
- distractions
- incomplete messages
- ambiguous wording
- lack of credibility
- lack of rapport
- taking disagreements on personal terms
- jargon
- boredom

Most educators and leaders I know would call these distractions a normal part of their meeting environment. Perhaps if we viewed these common communication distortions as potentially fatal errors, we would take them more seriously.

Constructive disagreements stem from a diversity of viewpoints, as leaders include not only experts in assessment and data analysis but also in curriculum, instruction, technology, leadership, and the emotional well-being of students and staff. Because most groups prize harmony over disagreement, it is essential that they create systems to insure divergent thinking. Therefore, the wise leader will insist on a discipline of mutually exclusive decision alternatives (D. Reeves, 2020b). The typical decision-making protocol for educational leaders is for the staff to make a recommendation and request the adoption of a single alternative. This process provides the illusion of unanimity and shields the superintendent and school board from some of the most important elements of the decision-making process: the consideration of alternatives, along with the advantages and disadvantages of each. Rather than bringing a single recommendation to the superintendent or principal on difficult issues, the staff should have at least two alternatives that are mutually exclusive, with each accompanied by advantages and disadvantages. The cabinet or school leadership team would serve the district and school better if, before the meeting, each member read and thought about a crisp memorandum—no longer than one or two pages—that had decision recommendations with pros and cons. Every option has disadvantages and risks. Leaders never make perfect decisions, but they can choose thoughtfully among alternative risks. Most senior school administrators I know are not accustomed to considering alternatives because that requires disagreement among the cabinet members. Brainwashed into the need for "buy-in," participants conceal disagreement behind a façade of gentility.

Consider, however, a decision that with the benefit of hindsight you now recognize as a poor one. Perhaps it was a technology acquisition, instructional initiative, or hiring decision. Would the bad decision have been avoided, or at least modified, if you had at least one clear alternative and if the cabinet or leadership team had a clear-eyed view of the advantages and disadvantages of the decision it made? The discipline of mutually exclusive options is especially important when committees or task forces make recommendations to the leader. When only a single alternative is presented, it is difficult for the superintendent or principal to do anything but accept the apparently unanimous recommendation of the group. We must remember, however, that these recommendations are rarely unanimous, and if they were, it could reflect insufficient exploration of alternatives and inadequate consideration of advantages and disadvantages.

THE CHALLENGES AND OPPORTUNITIES OF HIERARCHY

Earlier in this chapter we considered how hierarchy can inhibit communication, sometimes with fatal results. That should not imply, however, that a lack of hierarchical structure is the key to success. Educational organizations need a sense of organizational structure, and students, staff, and governing board members must understand how communication flows and how decisions are made. How can we balance the need for effective communication throughout the organization without chaos and confusion? Research on innovation in hierarchical organizations suggests ways that some of the most innovative organizations in the world, like the design company IDEO, can nevertheless have discipline and structure (Sanner & Bunderson, 2018). Specifically, it suggests that establishing some boundaries for potential solutions is an important contributor to effective innovation. Many readers have experienced traditional brainstorming sessions in which participants were encouraged to express every idea, no matter how absurd, and in no case render any judgment about the ideas of others. This process, started in the 1940s by advertising executive Alex Osborne, has been widely discredited (D. Reeves & Reeves, 2016). Traditional brainstorming processes undervalue the ideas of introverts who think more than they talk, but who may have far more creative ideas (Allen, 2018). Although idea generation can certainly be a messy process, it is not without structure and the need for convergence around the best available solutions. Moreover, one of the greatest limits of strict hierarchies—the failure of well-informed people who are lower in the organizational structure to speak up—can be addressed by effective disciplines that encourage and even require broad participation. Paradoxically, a well-crafted hierarchy can establish decision processes that encourage divergent points of view and send the clear message that universal agreement with the prevailing winds of advocacy can render a person irrelevant. In order to make hierarchies work, there must be a clear chain of command. This stops teams from going down rabbit holes and chasing pipe dreams and focuses organization resources and intellectual energy. Effective hierarchies can also focus on the results of team success rather than inadvertently pitting one person against the other in a culture of winners and losers.

In this chapter we have addressed the fact that building trust is not enough for fearless schools. Leaders and every stakeholder, including students, staff, and governing board members, must make a consistent commitment to maintaining trust. This includes a rhythm of promises made and promises kept, and open confession of when we miss the mark or fail to deliver on a promise. An inherent quality of a fearless school is leadership team members who are willing to listen—just listen—without advice, judgment, or interruption. It is one of the most frustrating and time-consuming, but absolutely essential, tasks of leadership. We considered the case for candor, acknowledging that candor can be unpleasant in some cases but far better than the alternatives in which leaders fail to provide performance feedback with the excuse of caring too much for the individuals. While radical candor does not support being a jerk, neither does it support the notion of killing the careers of colleagues with kindness. Fearless schools not only accept disagreement but also encourage it. They know the value of divergent thinking and will, when necessary, assign people to find advantages and disadvantages for different mutually exclusive decision alternatives. This is the opposite of the superficially harmonious agreement in which the leader is given only a "take it or leave it" alternative. Lastly, we considered the challenges and opportunities of hierarchy. The leadership literature on trust can be misinterpreted to imply that hierarchy is the enemy. In actual fact, stultifying and intransigent hierarchy is destructive. But a thoughtful hierarchy, as fearless schools can provide, can simultaneously encourage innovation and creativity while at the same time maintaining the guidance and leadership support necessary to turn ideas into action. We now turn our attention to the dark side of leadership, and how trust is destroyed in fearful schools.

DISCUSSION QUESTIONS

1. Think of an instance in which a leader or an organization clearly demonstrated that they kept the promises they made. Please describe the promise and exactly how you knew that it was kept. Describe your feelings and attitudes toward that leader or organization.

2. Find a partner—either live in your discussion group or by phone or other voice technology—and have a timer handy and do the following: "I'm doing an exercise for a book study, and I just want you to tell me about anything, and I will listen without interrupting you for two minutes. OK? Let's begin." Then start the timer and listen. Just listen. Notice your feelings at one minute, at 90 seconds, and finally at two minutes. What happened? Did you really remain silent? What happened when the other person stopped stalking

before the two minutes had passed—did you allow the silence to continue, or did you speak to fill in the awkward void? What insights did you gain from this two-minute exercise?

3. Kim Scott suggests that every coaching and feedback conversation takes place in one of four quadrants based on our focus on personal care for the individual and our focus on results. The four quadrants are: compassionate candor (high care, high performance), obnoxious aggression (low care, high performance), manipulative insincerity (low care, low performance), and ruinous empathy (high care, low performance). Think of a time when you have received coaching, feedback, or evaluative comments from a colleague or evaluator. Which quadrant best describes your conversation?

4. Now think of a future instance in which you will be providing coaching and feedback to someone else. What specifically do you need to do to provide compassionate candor—that is, high care for the individual and also deep commitment to performance?

5. How is divergent thinking suppressed in your organization? Consider the list of characteristics of doomed airline flights:
   - noise
   - multiple communications happening at once
   - fatigue, stress
   - distractions
   - incomplete message
   - ambiguous wording
   - lack of credibility
   - lack of rapport
   - taking disagreements in personal terms
   - jargon
   - boring

   How do any of these characteristics describe meetings you

recently attended? What can you to do make meetings more productive and to honor the value of divergent thinking?

6. If there is no apparent dissent in your team, what can you do to bring out constructive advocacy of divergent points of view?

7. Think of a time when you have engaged in a brainstorming activity. Based on what you learned in this chapter, how can you improve idea generation in your team or organization?

CHAPTER 4.

HOW TRUST IS DESTROYED

———————

In this chapter—

S ISYPHUS CHEATED DEATH, TWICE escaping Hades. His eternal punishment decreed by Zeus was to begin each day rolling a boulder up a hill from the depths of the underworld and, just as he reached the summit, the boulder would fall back down the hill. Every day for eternity, or at least until the retirement system kicked in, he would repeat the pointless exercise. Pointless repetition, endless futility, exhaustion, and never reaching impossible goals—another day in the life of many educational leaders and teachers. They begin each day hearing the demands and sometimes the encouragement of leaders and policymakers. "You can do it!" they yell. "Push that boulder up the hill! Failure is not an option!" But these voices ring hollow as they require action without the resources, time, and flexibility to meet the needs of every student. Nevertheless, teachers and leaders push the boulders uphill, making progress against all odds, and can succeed—the top of the hill is in sight. And then comes another broken promise, another burdensome rule, another insult, and another puncture in what had seemed to be the impenetrable armor of professional respect. This is how trust is destroyed, and how fearless teachers and leaders are turned into cynical, fearful, and emotionally devastated humans.

THE BURDENS OF PREVIOUS EXPERIENCES

We all approach decisions with bias. It is pervasive and ingrained, and to deny bias is to deny the reality of our culture and background. For example, there is a pervasive bias for tall people in leadership selection. Although only 15 percent of the population is over six feet tall, 58 percent of U.S. CEOs are at or above that height. Only 4 percent of the population is taller than six foot two; 33 percent of CEOs are at or above that height (Huang, 2020). These variations are far outside of the realm of random variation and reflect clear and consistent bias. Researchers also find bias against men, especially in the hiring of teachers. In a study of a Philadelphia area district, male teachers were paid less than female applicants and received less credit for prior experience. Interviews revealed anti-male bias, with questions such as "Why do you even want to work with kids?" Sometimes these biases take on extreme consequences, such as the finding that African American women are three to four times less likely to receive the medical care, including advanced procedures, that they need compared to their white counterparts with similar illnesses.

No one, no matter their background and role models, is

immune from the assumptions and biases that are pervasive in our culture. When a distinguished Stanford professor, an internationally known African American woman with particular expertise in cultural biases, was sitting in an airplane with her five-year-old son, an African American man was walking down the aisle, and the boy asked, "Mommy, is that man going to rob the plane?" (Eberstadt, 2020). If that young child, despite being raised with positive African American role models, can express such clear presumptions, then it does not ring true when well-intentioned people claim, "I just don't see color." We cannot eliminate bias and cultural assumptions, but we can use systems that help to diminish the impact of these prejudices. For example, when professional symphonies started having players perform their auditions behind a curtain so that only the music—not the appearance of the musician—matters, there was a striking increase in the number of women hired for spots in symphony orchestras (Eberstadt, 2020). Similarly, resumes and job applications can be viewed without names or other details that identify ethnicity and gender.

Huang (2020) suggests that we should not hate the player, but hate the game. We should understand that people in power have benefitted from the current system. They justify the system in place, they believe that the system is an unbiased meritocracy because, of course, they deserved their success. The answer is not more bias training, and some evidence suggests that many training programs actually result in worse performance by the managers who are supposed to show less bias in their decision-making. Consider the case of schools that have stopped requiring the SAT or ACT as tests of admission because they believe that these tests are biased against economically disadvantaged students. They insist that they want to look at the whole student, not just scores. But here's the rub: Economically advantaged students can afford more sports, clubs, tutoring, and volunteer experiences. Even without the biased tests, they nevertheless have an edge that wealthy parents can provide.

Attempting to solve a deeply cultural challenge, such as implicit bias and institutional racism, with an ineffective and potentially counterproductive workshop is a misuse of professional learning time and resources. The entirely legitimate emphasis on racial diversity obscures the deeper issue of preparing teachers to support academic equity and reimagining structures that support equity. Current efforts for antibias training and similar workshops will not give teachers and schools what they need. Countless consultants and private firms have been hired by schools and districts throughout the country for support with the "problem" of diversity. Most of this work has disproportionately been focused on individual personal growth. Racism takes on four forms: individual, institutional, interpersonal, and ideological. While the current professional learning trends focus on the individual, students remain in systems and schools that have yet to address the power and influence of institutional racism. Namely, students remain in schools where there is consistent evidence of white-supremacist structures: scheduling, tracking, low expectations, discipline practices that disproportionately affect non-white males, limited rigor, single-story curricula, and rote memorization—to name a few. The underlying ideological premises of our educational systems have not been reconsidered. We are asking teachers to effect change in their outcomes without fully giving them the tools and the environment where they can function. (Stacy Scott and Día Bryant, personal conversation, May 3, 2020).

Until that elusive prejudice-free day comes, we need to help students create their own privilege. Hard work is essential, but many candidates for jobs, scholarships, college admissions, and graduate fellowships have a record of hard work, community service, and academic success. How do we help students and colleagues deal with the lingering effects of bias? We can help students and colleagues demonstrate that their hard work matters. That is, they work not only on their skills but also on how their skills are perceived by others. It is unhelpful to have a story of grievance and anger, and gaining advantage through sympathy is not a lasting condition. This is what Huang called creating an edge, a combination of skill, personality, and personal stories. The world will never be a perfect meritocracy, and decisions will be riddled with prejudice. The answer is the edge.

HOW LEADERSHIP MYTHOLOGY UNDERMINES TRUST

We idolize mythical leaders, from Richard Branson in business to George Washington in politics to George Patton in war, from Rev. Dr. Martin Luther King Jr. in the civil rights movement to Gloria Steinem in the women's rights movement. While we can admire the causes for which these leaders devoted their lives, we make a grave mistake when we focus on the person rather than the cause. Giving leaders adulation is sometimes cathartic, and exceptional leaders in every age deserve our respect and appreciation. But they are never quite the mythical heroes that we would like them to be, and our ultimate understanding of their frailties can distort our understanding of their contributions. Consider some practical guidelines in the assessment of mythological leaders and how we can balance respect and appreciation without having the mythology get in the way of trust. When the leader is a hero of mythological proportions, then the rest of us are merely human. And humans can never compete with the gods. Just ask Sisyphus. Fortunately, we no longer worship Zeus. We can learn from and respect leaders without worshiping them.

There is another lesson from mythology, often misunderstood, and that is the tale of Icarus, the son of Daedalus (Godin, 2012). What most people remember about this tale is that Icarus was given wings, along with the instruction from his father not to fly too high, lest the sun melt his wings. The son's failure to follow his father's admonition led to him soaring too close to the sun, which melted his wings and plunged him into what is today known as the Icarian Sea. His death is a reminder to us all not to fly too high, lest our hubris leads to our demise. But that is only half the tale. Daedalus also told his son not to fly too low, lest his wings become soaked and he lose his ability to fly. When we recall the first half the myth without the second half, we associate ambition with death and mediocrity with safety. The full tale of Icarus reminds us that mediocrity, like hubris, can also be fatal—the death is just a lot slower. When we accept leadership mythology, we not only avoid hubris but we also lose the ability to learn from leadership successes. There is a difference between the danger zone, water that is too deep with uncertain currents— and the comfort zone, the shallow end of the pool where our feet can safety touch the ground. Between the danger zone and comfort zone lies the opportunity for growth. Jumping past the danger zone is ridiculous speculation. Past the comfort zone, by contrast, is the path of learning, experimentation, disappointment, success, and the growth that only happens with failure and feedback. It is not physical resources but trust, connection, and surprise that are the scarcest commodities in the 21st century (Godin, 2012).

Why do leadership myths persist? Because they serve the purpose of explaining the otherwise unexplainable. They confer upon an individual leader with magical gifts the outcomes that we seek. Thus, we revere the "Founding Fathers" rather than the sacrifice of thousands of unknown soldiers, mothers, sisters, and families. We believe that "Lincoln saved the Union," rather than the untold commitment of anonymous citizens and cities ravaged by war. In a comprehensive study of leaders from ancient times to the present, scholars found three prevalent myths: formulaic, attribution, and results (McChrystal et al., 2018).

The formulaic myth is based on our striving to understand the process of leadership. We seek a checklist so that we can replicate in today's environment the leadership successes of old. Thus, we have the risible and wildly inaccurate book, *The Leadership Secrets of Attila the Hun* (Roberts, 1990) and several less toxic but equally unreliable leadership formulas based on historical models that not only were not as successful as we would imagine but whose historical context is also deeply inconsistent with 21st-century reality. The attribution myth presumes that a single person, like Caesar, George Washington, Rev. Dr. Martin Luther King Jr., Susan B. Anthony, Winston Churchill, Mahatma Gandhi, or Vladimir Lenin—to name a few—were singularly responsible for their victories. But serious students of history know that the attribution myth is an oversimplification of complex reality. The third myth is the results myth, in which we commit the classical logical error of *post hoc, ergo propter hoc* (after this, therefore because of this). In other words, the leader who happens to be at the right place at the right time when victory happened, when popular opinion turned, or when the economy recovered was presumed to have caused those results. The results myth is pervasive in education, in which the charismatic teacher or leader who is in place when high test scores occurred was the sole cause of those scores. But every fourth-grade teacher knows that the reading proficiency of their students was a result of many causes, including not only teachers from kindergarten through third grade but also the degree to which the students were read to since infancy. Similarly, managers of teacher retirement portfolios are quick to take credit for a bull market in which a blindly-chosen mix of securities did well, a reflection of economic circumstances rather than the genius and insight of the portfolio manager. When results turn sour, then educators, leaders, and financiers quickly point to external causes that are beyond their control.

These three myths—formulaic myths, attribution myths, and results myths—form the basis for widespread misunderstanding of leadership. They also explain why, when the myths are proven baseless, we lose trust not only in the unmasked leader but also in the system for which the leader was responsible. It is not the flawed political leader who is taken down, but the entire political system that is regarded as corrupt and rigged. When educational leaders fail, the illogical conclusion is not that a single educational leader is flawed but that the public education system in general is flawed and must be dismantled. Myths leave in their wake a path of destruction, disinformation, and despair. The most difficult time to challenge a myth is when things are looking great. We want our heroes to be perfect, even when we know they are flawed. We want simple explanations for success of organizations, schools, armies, and markets, even when we know that success has many parents and the complexity of shared ownership requires a degree of humility that is difficult for leaders to exhibit, especially when times are good. It is far easier to share blame than credit.

The lazy inference of leadership myths is that there are only two categories of leaders: the strong and the weak, the former inevitably preferred. This false dichotomy leads to unquestioning submission and autocracy and is the opposite of the characteristics that are most important in leadership: integrity, intelligence, judgment, inquiry, willingness to seek disparate views, flexibility, courage, vision, empathy, and energy (Brow, 2014). But leadership is not weightlifting, in which the strong are always superior to the weak. Nuance, judgment, and a willingness to listen are not weaknesses but are at the very core of effective leadership. We do not need superheroes with superhuman strength and powers. Rather, we need leaders who are capable of understanding their own weaknesses and admitting their own errors.

It is not only leadership mythology that destroys trust. Even the best leaders, modest in their demeanor and well-intentioned in their actions, can fall victim to miscommunication brought on by inaccurate and incomplete information. This can lead to false hope by followers who have the fortitude to withstand bad news, but who do not have the patience for inaccurate and incomplete information, even when well-intended. Trust is not destroyed by challenge but by the failure to challenge with timely truth.

HOW INACCURATE AND INCOMPLETE INFORMATION DESTROYS TRUST

We know what accurate and timely information sounds like. While most readers of this book were not alive during the World War II, they have almost certainly heard Winston Churchill's admonition in the dark early days of that war that he had nothing to offer the people of Great Britain but blood, toil, tears, and sweat (Larson, 2020). Readers certainly will recall the warnings of the most visible member of the Coronavirus Task Force, Dr. Anthony Fauci, in the spring of 2020 (Faueh, 2020). These assessments spanning crises of the 20th and 21st centuries illustrate the value of credible, accurate and yes, scary, information. Contrast Churchill's candor with the illusions of his predecessor, who believed that Hitler was a man he could do business with and promised, with the sacrifice of Czechoslovakia, peace in our time. Contrast Fauci's candor with the promises of miracle cures for COVID-19 that led to the deaths of thousands who preferred mythical leadership to myth-busting facts (Marchione, 2020).

Inaccurate and incomplete information is not necessarily malicious. Leaders operate with the best information available to them, and in general they do not mislead their followers deliberately. Moreover, we tend to prefer optimistic leaders and people. The medical evidence is clear that optimistic people enjoy better physical and mental health, have healthier lifestyles, and better social connections (Conversano et al., 2010). But optimism has its dark side, especially in leadership. When leaders express the view that "We can do anything!" and "It can't be that hard—we've got the best people and can overcome any obstacle," their optimism can strike subordinates as naïve (Fessler, 2018). Worse yet, it sends the signal that the boss doesn't want to hear bad news. They want to hear "Pay no attention to that bit of ice in the ocean" rather than "Iceberg ahead! Turn hard to starboard!" They certainly don't want to hear that the budget for time and resources was underestimated and that the project might fail. While we admire the can-do spirit of the NASA engineers and astronauts who saved the Apollo 11 mission, we fail to recognize that real rocket scientists fail a great many more times than they succeed. It is their persistent failures and their ability to learn from those failures, including tragic ones, which allow for the successes (Varol, 2020). While the optimist intends to cheer people up and to motivate them, the leaders whose optimism blinds them to reality unintentionally diminish their followers, making them feel incompetent and unsafe. Our followers, including not only direct reports in the organization, but all stakeholders, can handle the truth. In schools, for example, we conduct fire drills because we want students and staff members to act responsibly during an emergency, neither denying that a fire is a very real threat nor panicking and descending into chaos. The same is true when we take on other challenges, from serving students in poverty to dealing with the challenges of poor housing and medical care, to a fundamental lack of safety. These, along with inadequate literacy skills, are the serious challenges that teachers and leaders face every day. Saying to teachers and students, "Just work hard enough and a miracle will happen" does not motivate them but makes them think instead that only miracles, rather than personal agency, will serve them well. Students and staff members need hope, not fantasies. They need realistic support and communication that the real challenges they face require solutions that are difficult, but not Sisyphean. The boulders they move are heavy—but not unmovable. The hills are steep—but not endless. That is the balance that leaders must achieve, communicating with honesty and realism. It is encouragement, not fear, that motivates individuals and teams. When people feel that their failure to achieve goals is the result of their own incompetence or lack of sufficient effort, they fear the psychological punishment that inevitably follows. Sometimes that punishment is inflicted by others, and sometimes by themselves. But in either case, punishment never achieves the desired result.

HOW PUNISHMENT DESTROYS TRUST

Literature provides rich examples of the futility of punishment, whether self-imposed, as in *Crime and Punishment*'s Raskolnikov (Dostoevsky, 1866) or imposed by an anonymous irrational actor in *The Trial* (Kafka, 1925). But we don't need literary terror to recognize the futility of punishment. It doesn't work for pets (Tynes, n.d.), it doesn't work for children (Karson, 2014), it doesn't work for criminals (Kelly, 2018). In fact, decades of being tough on crime have given the US a higher incarceration rate than totalitarian regimes such as Russia or the former white supremacist government of Rhodesia. Our zeal for punishment is irrational, particularly in the face of international evidence that there are alternatives to punishment that are better for society in every respect.

The readers of this book are largely educators and educational leaders, and perhaps a few can remember the days of swats on the buttocks or hands administered for misbehavior. It might surprise you to know that as of the spring of 2020, 19 states continue to permit corporal punishment (Kennedy, 2020). In one of the most stunning examples of deliberate and persistent indifference to evidence, school administrators and policy makers permit this barbaric practice more than a half a century after definitive evidence that corporal punishment was ineffective and counterproductive. A synthesis of more than 250 studies over more than 50 years (Global Initiative to End All Corporal Punishment of Children, 2016) concluded that corporal punishment of students resulted in, among other effects,

- externalizing behavior problems in childhood;
- internalizing behavior problems in childhood;
- impaired cognitive activity in childhood;
- low self-esteem in childhood;
- holding positive attitudes about "spanking" as an adult.

It is not just the children who receive punishment but those who witness it as well.

Few leaders today actually beat their subordinates, though some workers might prefer a beating to the sadistic humiliations to which some managers subject them. Even the terminology used to describe verbal assaults—*ripping a new one, raking over the coals*—reveals a zest for punishment that is deeply ingrained. While we know that discipline is important, the term "discipline" shares the same root as "disciple"—a learner. The question, therefore, is not whether children or adults deserve punishment.

Rather, the question is: how do they best learn? That is the one and only point of discipline. People of all ages learn through example, modeling, affirmation, encouragement, feedback, and correction. They do not learn anything of value through punishment, except to fear whatever actions or attempted actions were punishment. If toddlers were punished for every fall, they would never learn to walk because they would never attempt any action that might lead to another fall. If novice pianists are rapped on the wrists for every wrong note, they will never progress beyond "Chopsticks" because that, and only that, can be performed with perfection. In schools, teachers will never try new technology, new means of student engagement, new methods of assessment, or any idea that might lead to better pedagogy and learning if the result of their experimentation and inevitable failures along the way are administrative punishments ranging from a poor evaluation to a look of disdain, to a verbal humiliation in front of colleagues. Punishment undermines trust, and it is the foremost threat to learning in any classroom, faculty meeting, professional learning community, cabinet meeting, or board room.

A punishment-free environment does not imply the absence of consequences for bad actions. Feedback that is timely and accurate is essential for adults and students. Consequences for actions that are dangerous, inappropriate, and wrong can and must include removal from the classroom or the building. When a student has a weapon, they must be disarmed and dismissed. When adults engage in sexual misconduct or threaten or otherwise harm a student, they must be removed. But the vast majority of punishments in schools are not for these grave offenses. I have examined hundreds of referrals for student misconduct. The primary offenses are failure to complete work, disrespect, and failure to follow instructions. None of these infractions are diminished by trips to the office. In fact, when students are disengaged from classwork and sent down the hallway, it is not a punishment at all, it is a reward. And if the punishment includes verbal humiliation and thinly veiled physical threats, the only certain result is one more child who hates school and everyone in it. Similarly, when leaders punish staff members, they must be ready to deal with the consequences of insidious disruption that is toxic to every department, school, and system.

To be sure, some staff members require removal, and effective leaders document the case and make the removal swift and legally defensible. But far more common is the death by a thousand cuts with years of verbal warnings, then written reprimands, then relenting—and the cycle continues, devastating the morale of the staff members who are working hard to make a difference. We dare not conflate ineffective punishment, such as reprimands and humiliations, with effective and necessary consequences, such as completing assigned work and appropriate constraints on student activities. The latter is too seldom used, and the former is far too frequent.

So let there be no mistake: The case against punishment is not a case against discipline or necessary removals of students and adults for safety reasons. But the half-hearted imposition of authority through punishments simply doesn't work. Teachers need to be able to deal with disrespect and unfinished work in the classroom, just as administrators must deal with catcalls and disrespectful dialogue in a faculty meeting. In sum, if actions threaten the safety of the children and adults for whom we are responsible, then remove them. If their behavior is obnoxious and unpleasant, then confront it, model and reward better alternatives, and improve the individual and collective performance of the group.

FALSUS IN UNO, FALSUS IN OMNIBUS

Leaders are forgiven for many mistakes. They will misunderstand data. They will underestimate challenges. They will overestimate their ability to handle these challenges. And for these and many other mistakes, they will be forgiven if, and only if, they are trustworthy. But a single breach of trust will lead to the Latin proverb, *falsus in uno, falsus in omnibus* (false in one thing, false in everything). Perfection is not required, but absolute integrity requires the prohibition of the passive voice in dealing with error. It is never "mistakes were made"; rather, it is "I was wrong and accept complete responsibility for this mistake." This sort of personal accountability is so rare in American leadership. Perhaps it is because leaders attained their lofty positions due to the presumption of invulnerability and, having been elevated to a leadership position, are now unable to acknowledge responsibility for mistakes. But whatever the source of this imperviousness to accountability, it is a fatal flaw for leaders. A lie—especially a deliberate lie—threatens their credibility in all things great and small.

The threats to integrity that plague our educational systems begin in the classroom and home. Evidence suggests that more than half of high school students have admitted cheating on tests and almost two-thirds acknowledged plagiarism (Simmons, 2018). These are not students typically categorized as delinquents but those in competitive high schools—students with well-educated parents and young people who aspire to be successful in college and beyond. Their rationalizations run the gamut from desiring to help others in need to unrealistic parental expectations. But the real root of the rationalizations is that "everybody does it"—including adults in leadership positions. While there are increasingly sophisticated efforts to catch cheaters and plagia-rizers, technology is not the antidote for the amoral calculus of deceit. That is a leadership issue, not a technological one.

In this chapter we considered the burdens of previous experi-ences and how everyone brings to their daily engagement with other humans the perspectives and memories associated with pre-vious encounters. If these previous recollections were tainted by mistrust, then it requires exceptional effort by leaders to establish and maintain trust. We are not served well by leadership myths in which we idolize heroes rather than humanize them. We can respect and admire leaders in history and in our own day without falling victim to false portraits of their infallibility. Information is the stock-in-trade of leaders, provided that the information they dispense is accurate and complete. When leaders share only the glitter but not the granite, they are signaling that they distrust the people they aspire to lead. Trust is destroyed with every bit of information that sugarcoats reality. Leaders destroy trust with punishment, whether physical, psychic, or interpersonal. Despite decades of evidence on the ineffectiveness and destructive nature of punishment, it still remains a fixture of the educational system from the kindergarten classroom to the highest levels of leader-ship. Finally, we considered the impact of a single lie, the sin-gle act of deceit upon the credibility of leaders and their ability to function. In matters large and small, leaders must represent absolute integrity in order to have the support of students, staff, and stakeholders when the going is tough. They must, in sum, be fearless enough to deal with unpleasant and difficult truths, knowing that those whom they lead are sufficiently fearless to hear it.

In Part II we will consider resilience and how fearless schools can bounce back from even the most devasting disappointments.

Of all the gifts that we give to our students and colleagues, resilience is the one that will last a lifetime and be there when they need it most.

DISCUSSION QUESTIONS

1. How have your previous experiences with misplaced trust in professional or personal life influenced your view of your current organization and leadership?

2. How, in your experience, have leaders been mythologized? What super-powers did you or colleagues attribute to leaders? How did you discover that the myth was not true?

3. Reflect on the role that punishment has played in your life, from childhood to your professional life. Think of when punishment might have motivated you and how it might have undermined your motivation. Please describe the circumstances, how punishment was administered, and what the results were.

4. In your role now—as a professional, parent, or colleague—how do you provide coaching and feedback that does not carry with it the negative aspects of punishment?

5. Think of a time when the Latin proverb *falsus in uno, falsus in omnibus* applied to your views of leaders or colleagues in your organization. What was the one thing that was false that led you to believe that everything from that source would also be false?

PART II:

RESILIENCE

ALTHOUGH THE TERM "RESILIENCE" is commonly used to describe the emotional strength to rebound from disappointment and failure, the term actually stems from metallurgy. This origin holds important clues for our consideration of individual and organizational resilience. Almost all materials have some degree of elasticity. This is true even of steel beams that form the foundation of 100-story buildings. If these apparently solid and unbendable beams did not have some elasticity, at the first shift in the ground—such as that associated with an earthquake—the beams would break apart and the building would come crashing down. If, on the other hand, the beams were too elastic, they would bend so far that the building would fall over. The challenge for structural engineers is to determine the "modulus of resilience" (Dipto, n.d.), the point at which a metal can bend and then return to its original shape. People and organizations, like steel beams, have their own modulus of resilience. If they are unable to bend at all, they will fall apart under stress. If they bend too much, they can no longer support the emotional loads they carry and are unable to return to their originally strong condition. In the following chapters, we will first consider physical resilience, how our bodies can sustain damage and nevertheless bounce back from pressure. Next, we will consider emotional resilience and how loss, despair, loneliness, and other emotional injuries can be devastating yet survivable. Then we will consider organizational resilience. Just like the human body, organizations can suffer diminished resilience with age. However, just as with physical and emotional resilience, organizations can also bounce back from the disruption of challenge and change.

CHAPTER 5

PHYSICAL RESILIENCE

In this chapter—
- Bouncing Back from Physical and Psychic Injury
- Bouncing Back from Illness
- Bouncing Back from Exhaustion
- Bouncing Back from Fear

THE CLINICAL DEFINITION OF resilience is intimidating:

> Physical resilience is the ability of an organism to respond to stressors that acutely disrupt normal physiological homeostasis. By definition, resilience decreases with increasing age, while frailty, defined as a decline in tissue function, increases with increasing age. (Schorr et al., 2017.)

We often associate physical resilience with athletes who have recovered from an injury on the field of play; a cancer survivor; or a person suffering traumatic brain injury who, through a combination of exceptional medical care and personal determination, was able to overcome great odds to walk, talk, and think again. While these examples may offer a degree of inspiration, the problem with heroism as a model is that it is not sustainable. It is the same problem that we discussed in the previous chapter concerning heroic leaders. It is too easy to lapse into all-or-nothing thinking, in which the gulf between heroism and abject defeat cannot be spanned. But most of us are not professional athletes, nor do we have access to an army of treatment providers who are there to support the success stories of heroic recoveries. This chapter is for the rest of us.

BOUNCING BACK FROM PHYSICAL AND PSYCHIC INJURY

Resilience involves both physical and mental capacities—strength, endurance, and perseverance. These qualities are essential to any recovery, whether it is recovery from an accident on a bicycle, recovery from depression and anxiety, recovery from addiction, or recovery from the loss of a loved one or relationship. While each of these situations may seem strikingly different, the keys to resilience in each of them have much in common. The same is true for the disappointment that students feel after the many losses that occur in schools—loss of friendships, loss of teachers they love at the end of each school year, and the loss of self-confidence that occurs after an academic setback or competitive defeat. The lessons of physical resilience are helpful in all these cases.

When athletes suffer an injury and are sidelined from their sport, they often suffer a loss of identity. They can feel purposeless without the training and competition to which they are accustomed (Kuzma & Jackson Cheadle, 2019). If my identity is as "Sara's boyfriend" or "ace math student," or "Mom's favorite," then anything that deprives me of this identity can be mentally and physically devastating. In cases of addiction, some people are chemically dependent upon alcohol or drugs. But far more common are the cases in which the persistent and damaging use of addictive substances serves a psychological need to feel important, impressive, and good-looking. Indeed, there is a high degree of comorbidity in which people who abuse alcohol and drugs also suffer from disorders involving stress, anxiety, and depression (National Institute on Drug Abuse, 2010). While few people think of cigarettes as glamorous in the 21st century, it was difficult to find an admired character in movies, business, journalism, or political leadership who did not have a cigarette, cigar, or pipe close at hand in the mid-20th century. Half a century later, it is easy to see the horrible effects of tobacco, alcohol, and drug abuse—but also impossible to forget the images of the martini-swilling executive, cocaine-snorting rock star, and Adderall-addicted coworker or high-performing student. When we are ultimately required to give up the alcohol, cocaine, Adderall, or other substances—we not only suffer physically, as injured athletes do, but we also suffer the same loss of identity. How can I be an ace student or star performer without a stimulant? How can I be popular without alcohol? Lessons from physical resilience can be exceptionally helpful to those requiring psychological resilience.

Trainers and other treatment providers (Kuzma & Jackson Cheadle, 2019) who have supported athletes after several physical injuries understand the intersection of physical and psychic resilience. Their regimen includes the following steps: First, set small goals. For the athlete who has suffered a catastrophic injury, a goal might be the ability to wiggle one's toes. For the endurance athlete, that may not seem like much, but for the person facing a lifetime of paralysis without feeling below the chest, the restoration of movement and feeling in the toes is an immensely satisfying accomplishment. I know from personal experience that after completing the 2012 Boston Marathon in record-high heat, the ability to walk without assistance the following day seemed like once again crossing the finish line on Commonwealth Avenue. I learned to never again be impatient with people who stand on the moving walkways of airports, as I surely needed mechanical assistance during those post-marathon days.

The second key to resilience is structure. Not only do those recovering from physical injury require structure, but so do those dealing with psychological challenges. During the global shutdown in the midst of the COVID-19 pandemic, psychologists reported significant differences between families that maintained a consistent structure—breakfast, school, work, dinner, games, and safe walks—compared to those who allowed the shutdown to paralyze them into indolence and chaos (Clark, 2020).

Third, resilience requires the anticipation of setbacks. Athletes trip, addicts relapse, teachers who vowed never to raise their voice lose their temper. They are tested just one too many times, and their resolutions for performance or serenity go up in flames. These setbacks are neither moral failings nor character flaws. They are part of resilience. The anticipation of setbacks does not justify letting one's guard down and accepting failure as inevitable. Setbacks are not failures, provided we acknowledge them and move on. When riders fall off the horse, they get back on immediately. When pilots have a rough landing, they learn from it, ensure that they are physically and mentally safe to fly, and then get back in the left seat and take command of the aircraft. When addicts take a drink, they do not excuse it, but neither do they perseverate about it. They just get back on the journey to recovery.

The fourth and most difficult part of resilience is accountability. High-performing students and adults prize their independence. Their wishes for themselves are expressed in the words of the poem *Invictus*:

> I am the master of my fate,
> I am the captain of my soul. (Henley, 1888)

And who could be against such self-reliance, a virtue extolled by Emerson's essay of that name and by McGuffey's Readers, used from the 1830s well into the 20th century. Students in elementary grades (McGuffey, 1879) were instructed that where there is a will, there is a way. Not only were the behavioral and attitudinal standards established by McGuffey (whose hold on education lasted more than a century) exceptional, but a 21st-century analysis of the reading level of these volumes also reveals a remarkable level of academic expectations. In my own review of *McGuffey's Third Eclectic Reader* for example, I found that modern reading-level analytical tools suggest that what was expected of third-graders in the 19th century is regarded as ninth-grade reading level in the 21st century (D. B. Reeves, 2010).

The fifth element of physical resilience is celebrating accomplishments. For people who have run marathons and then were injured, it can seem trivial to celebrate running or even walking a single mile. But ask any first-time marathoner, and they will tell you that they did not wake up one day and complete a 26.2-mile course. They built their strength and endurance one mile at a time. They learned not only about the mechanics of running but also about hydration, nutrition, contingency planning, and the value of feedback. This focus on incremental gains is at the heart of success in music, academics, athletics, and relationships (Ericsson & Pool, 2016). Repudiating the superficiality of the 10,000-hour rule, which suggests that one can become an expert at something after practicing it for 10,000 hours, researchers found that resilience and performance come not from the quantity of practice but from the manner in which the practice is conducted. Deliberate practice involves breaking down each step—whether it's a *grand plié* in ballet, a perfect scale on the violin, or the essential movement of each foot strike in the runner—and it is the identification and celebration of incremental successes on which resilience and ultimate success depends. If 10,000 hours were all that were required for success, then we would not witness the typical scene on the golf course in which the duffer at age 65 has the same handicap as at age 25. Forty years of practice—a lot more than 10,000 hours—yields nothing without deliberate attention to detail.

These five elements of bouncing back from physical and psychic injury—small goals, structure, anticipating setbacks, accountability, and celebration—are essential whether one is crawling back from an injury or conquering a crippling depression, running a marathon or breaking through writer's block, losing weight or abandoning addictive substances. Recovery is never a straight line, and while discipline is essential, perfection is not.

BOUNCING BACK FROM ILLNESS

Harvard Medical School Professor Julie Silver (Harvard Women's Health Watch, 2012) notes that while recovery from severe illnesses, like cancer, have much in common with recovery from injury, patients with these illnesses are rarely treated the way recovery athletes are. While athletes receive plans for both treatment and rehabilitation, patients recovering from severe illnesses typically find that their treatment ends with, well, treatment. A cancer survivor herself, Silver noted that even after successful treatment, she was enormously fatigued and continued to suffer pain. While athletes with head and neck injuries are treated both for pain and for improved range of motion in the neck, stroke and cancer patients with the same limitations rarely receive this level of continuous daily support.

The language of recovery is also strikingly different between injuries and illness. When recovering from injury, patients track their small wins and engage in deliberate practice to gauge improvements. People suffering from illnesses, by contrast, sometimes measure their degree of success in terms of the passage of time, such as cancer-free for two years. This perspective is that of the treatment provider rather than that of the patient, and it can lead to substantial disconnections between the patient and those providing medical support. There are certainly exceptions that test the rule, and in many parts of the country cancer patients band together as a team, much in the way that injured athletes do. But in many other cases, treatment of illness takes place in isolation, just as it does for those suffering from depression or debilitating anxiety. Not everyone benefits from a team or group, and it is fair to say, for example, that the scientific community is deeply divided on the efficacy of group treatment programs for addiction, such as 12-Step, Smart Recovery, and many variations on the theme (Glaser, 2015). What is clear, however, is that there are elements of physical and psychic resilience that can be helpfully applied to the context of recovery from illness.

BOUNCING BACK FROM EXHAUSTION

"Fatigue makes cowards of us all," a quote variously attributed to Green Bay Packers Coach Vince Lombardi, General George Patton, and even William Shakespeare; though the Bard, in

Hamlet, wrote "Conscience makes cowards of us all." Whatever the literary provenance of this truism about fatigue, it takes a real toll on humans of every age. Whenever one finds a fearful school, one is also likely to find a climate of fatigue. The students and teachers are not lazy, but they are exhausted beyond measure. The scientific literature shows that the impact of fatigue on work-related accidents, depression, sleep disorders, and mental illness is consistent and profound (Rose et al., 2017; SafeStart, 2020).

Chronic exhaustion is not cured with a nap or superficial advice to get more sleep. A comprehensive response to fatigue requires a combination of medical, psychological, and environmental adjustments. In order to rule out chronic medical conditions, such as sleep apnea, those who suffer from fatigue and exhaustion should consider a complete medical evaluation including a sleep study if recommended by their physician. Stress, anxiety, and depression can also be associated with fatigue, and a mental health care provider can conduct appropriate assessment and treatment for these conditions. Some of the simplest treatments for exhaustion, however, can occur with environmental changes in the workplace. Frequent breaks are not a sign of laziness but of a thoughtfully designed way to approach the mental and physical restoration we all need. Whether working on the factory floor, engineer's desk, financier's computer, or classroom, the vast majority of American workers need far more breaks than they are getting. This fatigue-inducing schedule is compounded by stale air—windows rarely open in office and factories to admit fresh air—food designed for lethargy rather than energy, and emotionally draining supervisors. Very small investments of time and resources into a healthier environment could reduce the physical and financial costs associated with the medical and personal days off that result from fatigue and exhaustion. And in the context of schools, a single missed day can affect the learning of hundreds of students and lead to a chain reaction of missed instruction, compressed testing, and anxiety telegraphed to students. Indeed, fatigue and exhaustion are highly communicable throughout every school.

BOUNCING BACK FROM FEAR

Fear, once instilled, is very difficult to shake. I have had an irrational fear of snakes and spiders since childhood. While I rationally know that the vast majority of snakes, especially the variety one finds in gardens, are not poisonous, I will literally yell with fear when I see one. I know that most spiders are not only harmless to humans, but are also essential workers in our gardens, yet I recoil from them. I have friends from India, where canines as pets are not common, who are deathly afraid of my utterly harmless, overweight dog, Artemis. My Kenyan friends explain that if the snake that bites me is a black mamba, I shouldn't bother calling the doctor, as I will soon die. And if it is not a black mamba, then I probably don't need to call the doctor. Neither of these statements intended to make me feel calmer about snakes has the desired effect. I am simply paralyzed, irrationally and completely, with fear about snakes and spiders. But like most people, I also carry around fears about people. From students and colleagues, there is chronic fear of criticism, fear of failing to meet their expectations, and fear of failing to help as much as needed or in the precise way that was necessary. Like many of my friends, I carry around the fear of disappointing my parents, even though my father died more than two decades ago and always offered unstinting support and affirmation. If this is the way that rational and well-educated adults respond to fear, let us consider the perspectives of students, first-year teachers, new administrators,

FEARLESS SCHOOLS

or those veteran colleagues who have seen the world of education and, indeed, the world at large change around them. All the assumptions they had made about everything—from their professional status to health, to financial security—is seemingly in doubt, and yet they are expected to carry on as bulwarks of stability in the sea of distress faced by students, family members, and colleagues. How, then, do we bounce back from fear? The answer lies not in pop psychology and well-intentioned encouragement, but in science.

Though the part of our brains that responds with fear is as ancient as our species, we do not need a predator fixated on making a meal out of us to experience gut-wrenching fear. But new research suggests that we can train our brains to moderate the fight-or-flight response and channel our energies more productively.

> Scientists can see how resilient brains respond to emotion differently, found Martin Paulus, scientific director and president of the Laureate Institute for Brain Research in Tulsa, Okla. In a series of brain-imaging experiments on resilient Navy SEALs, Paulus showed the SEALs a color cue that signaled they were about to see an emotional picture. Paulus saw that their brains anticipated the emotion more quickly than the average brain, letting them jump nimbly between different types of emotions. Paulus says that in his research he has seen differences in the brains of people with anxiety or depression that suggest they have a hard time letting go of emotions and are often too engaged in emotional processes. The Navy SEALs, on the other hand, weren't glued to the emotional experiences. Why? "They're more resilient," he says. And just like working your biceps or your abs, say experts, training your brain

can build up strength in the right places—and at the right times—too. (Oaklander, 2015)

You don't need to train as a Navy SEAL to improve your resilience. Research at the Yale School of Medicine suggests that facing things that scare us, along with a clear ethical code that guides decisions, can deflect the automatic resort to fear-based decisions. There is also promising research that suggests that physical exercise and mindfulness meditation are associated with improved levels of resilience and moderated responses to fear (Oaklander, 2015).

Evidence from medical researchers (Johnson, 2020) suggest three ways to build resilience. First, it is important to connect with other people, forming healthy relationships with family, friends, and others. This is difficult, but not impossible, to accomplish in a virtual environment. The key is that these are not utilitarian exchanges. You are not saying, "I'd like to get involved with you because it will help me be resilient." Rather, you are seeking connections because you are genuinely interested in other people, their causes, passions, and beliefs. Second, self-care is essential. In education, we tend to valorize the heroic teachers and leaders who burn themselves to a cinder in the service of their students. But heroism and the fatigue that inevitably follows repeated extraordinary exertion are not sustainable strategies, and the burned-out teacher and leader cannot help the students and schools they seek to serve. Self-care includes not only nutrition, exercise, and enjoyment but also judiciously turning off phones and other electronic connections in order to have uninterrupted time for contemplation and meditation. Third, regular progress toward meaningful goals is strongly linked to positive intrapersonal and interpersonal relationships. This is what two Harvard Business School professors call "the progress principle" (Amabile & Kramer, 2011). Small daily wins, the page of the manuscript, the single conversation with a colleague, the kind and unexpected gesture for a friend—these are the small things that create large quantities of resilience.

In this chapter we explored how people are resilient, bouncing back from physical and psychic injuries, illness, fatigue, and fear. There are strong consistencies in the research about resilience in the face of these obstacles. Just as the professional athlete can apply these lessons, so can the middle-school math teacher, a school superintendent, the kindergarten teacher of a certain age, or the families of all of these people. While we don't need the trainers and therapeutic support that professional athletes have, we do know that, incongruously, self-reliance does not occur in a solitary environment. The relationships, challenges, love, and support of others are keys to resilience from all the setbacks that life gives us. In the next chapter we learn that physical resilience provides a model for emotional resilience, the quality that is necessary from infancy to our final days. There is a symbiotic relationship between physical resilience and emotional resilience, with each supporting the other and each necessary to sustain the other.

DISCUSSION QUESTIONS

1. Think of a time when you, a loved one, or friend suffered a physical injury. Describe the path to recovery, both physically and mentally. What support systems were available to aid in recovery? Looking back, what could have made bouncing back from this injury less painful?

2. Professor Julie Silver noted some important differences in the supports offered to people recovering from illness and those bouncing back from an injury. In your own experience or

the experiences of friends and loved ones, what differences have you noticed between recovery from injury and recovery from illnesses?

3. Almost every educator and leader has suffered from exhaustion at some point. How do you cope with fatigue and exhaustion? What is some well-intended advice you have received that failed to work for you?

4. Almost everyone experiences some sort of fear. Think about a time when you experienced fear and how you recovered from it. What parts of resilience in the face of fear can you accomplish alone, and what parts require the support of other people?

CHAPTER 6.

EMOTIONAL RESILIENCE

In this chapter—
- Bouncing Back from Stress
- Bouncing Back from Anxiety
- Bouncing Back from Depression

THE REASON PHYSICAL RESILIENCE and emotional resilience are so intertwined is that the damage from continued stress, anxiety, and depression takes a physical toll. While people in helping professions—such as education, social work, and medical care—sometimes like to claim that they can just compartmentalize their lives and work through the stress associated with their jobs, the reports from nurses, teachers, physicians, and educational leaders suggest an entirely different reality. Research from the Mayo Clinic confirms that stress is related to headaches, muscle tension or pain, chest pain, fatigue, change in sex drive, upset stomach, and sleep problems (Mayo Clinic, 2019). In a clinical study, anxiety was associated with heart disease, and depression with asthma, persistent cough, hypertension, heart disease, and gastrointestinal problems (Kang et al., 2014). Fortunately, research sheds light not only on the debilitating impacts of stress, anxiety, and depression but also on ways to foster resilience.

BOUNCING BACK FROM STRESS

During the COVID-19 crisis in the spring of 2020, health care workers faced what a Harvard Medical School researcher called "stabbing a fresh wound" (Saleh, 2020). Not only were they taking on an extra workload with patients testing the capacity of hospitals, but health care workers were becoming ill themselves, reducing the professional staff available to support increasing quantities of patients with increasingly severe ailments. Moreover, physicians had to make heart-rending decisions about who would or would not receive life-saving treatment. China was several months ahead of the United States in facing these challenges, and their medical providers reported that 50.4 percent had symptoms of depression, 34 percent had insomnia, 44.6 percent had symptoms of anxiety, and 71.5 percent had distress. Similarly, teachers and school administrators have faced exceptionally stressful conditions. Surveys reveal that teacher morale declined dramatically and that the emotional toll taken by the students they see, especially by the students with whom they are not in contact, is devastating. (Gewertz, 2020) Simple tasks take longer in a virtual environment, and the individual attention on which students depend is sorely lacking, even in cases where students have access to computers and internet connectivity. In other cases, teachers attempted to reach students with individual phone calls and personal visits to homes, sometimes reaching students on sidewalks and driveways. In addition to the emotional stress that this caused, teachers soon exhibited physical symptoms of burnout, not surprising given that their workdays extended from the early morning hours until late at night. Although a good deal of this stress is due to the care that teachers, paraprofessionals, and administrators extend to their students, it is inescapable that with more than 92 percent of COVID-19 deaths affecting those age 55 and over, and almost 30 percent of the teaching population over age 50, concerns for personal health also contribute to teacher stress.

In order to bounce back from stress, professionals in education (Israel, 2015) and medicine (Saleh, 2020) receive strikingly similar advice. While not all these suggestions work for everyone, at least one or two ideas might be worthwhile for readers who need to have a systematic and thoughtful way to bound back from stress.

First, the source of resilience in the face of stress is our mission. Educators are mission-driven people. We got into this profession to make a difference for our students, for our colleagues, and for the world. When things are overwhelmingly stressful, it is worth recalling the students and families we have helped. I have friends who, during the COVID-19 shut down, have taken out keepsakes, such as pictures and letters from former students, to remind them of how important their work is. They are making personal calls to current and former students, and they are receiving notes and calls of appreciation—in the case of one of my friends, from a student who was in his class more than 40 years ago.

Second, we can bring to mind those times when our resilience brought us through exceptional challenges. As I interviewed people for this chapter, I found colleagues and friends who have bounced back from the stress associated with traumatic injury and subsequent rehabilitation, from the loss of family, and from the interruptions of the teaching and leadership careers that they loved. When huge parts of our lives are invested in the care of students and family members, the involuntary loss of these connections can lead to exceptional levels of stress that is manifested in many physical and psychological ways. Yet as people talked to me about their paths to resilience, there were common themes, principally focused on a sense of meaning and purpose that they had nurtured for a very long time, in many cases since childhood.

Third, focus on the present. In the life of every educator and leader there are two inboxes. One is filled with things we can control—the feedback we provide to students, the ways we engage with colleagues, the new ideas that we consider as experiments. The other inbox is filled with things we cannot control— the actions of colleagues, students, parents, and policymakers. Stress is elevated when we focus on the second inbox, and stress is moderated when we focus on the first inbox. Psychological researchers refer to the first inbox as internal locus of control and the second inbox as external locus of control (Cherry, 2019). People with internal locus of control

- tend to be less influenced by the opinions of other people;
- often do better at tasks when they are allowed to work at their own pace;
- usually have a strong sense of self-efficacy;
- tend to work hard to achieve the things they want;
- feel confident in the face of challenges;
- tend to be physically healthier;
- report being happier and more independent;
- often achieve greater success in the workplace.

By contrast, people with external locus of control

- blame outside forces for their circumstances;
- often credit luck or chance for any successes;
- don't believe that they can change their situation through their own efforts;

- frequently feel hopeless or powerless in the face of difficult situations;
- are more prone to experiencing learned helplessness.

Building an internal locus of control as a strategy to bounce back from stress requires a conscious coercion on a daily, even minute-by-minute, basis to choose to focus on the first inbox. Conversations, email chains, and meetings that lead you to perseverating on an external locus of control must be avoided. Your time and energy are limited and valuable, and you cannot invest these precious resources on matters that only serve to diminish your sense of personal power and agency.

The fourth way of bouncing back from stress is to practice gratitude. Some people keep a gratitude journal, while others simply begin the day by reflecting on the people and things for which they are grateful. A consistent sense of gratitude does not minimize the reality of the challenges around us, but it adds an important sense of perspective. When I was working in Zambia to support teachers and educational leaders, I visited a village where people were singing and dancing. My host told me that the song they were singing, nearly in ecstasy, contained the lyrics, "We are so grateful … we are so grateful." On the way to the next village, my guide informed me that the people singing this beautiful song in four-part harmony were patients at an HIV-AIDS clinic, all with dire prognoses. Their song rings in my ears to this day every time I am tempted by toxic self-pity or petty aggravation.

Stress is a reality for the vast majority of educators and leaders, but so is resilience. Bouncing back from stress requires a focus on our sense of mission. Children, families, colleagues, and communities depend on us, and thus we lead lives of meaning and purpose no matter the stressors of the day. Second, we can focus on the present. While we are not oblivious to the future, which is usually unpredictable, or the past, which is unchangeable, our greatest amount of emotional energy is devoted to the here and now. This is closely related to the third strategy of bouncing back from stress, and that is an internal locus of control. Every minute of the day we choose where to focus our physical, intellectual, and emotional energy. When that focus takes us to people and conditions beyond our control—the huge inbox of matters we can neither influence nor control—then we fall into a well of despair. When we choose to focus on the things we can control, then we can enjoy the psychological balm of the internal locus of control. Fourth, we bounce back from stress by practicing gratitude. We contemplate and express gratitude not only for the people and things around us but also for the memories of friends and loved ones of the past. While we can grieve losses, we can also remember with gratitude the people who have had a profound and positive influence on us. I recommend writing a letter to a teacher who had a profound influence on you, perhaps years or decades ago. It will brighten the day of that teacher and it will also help you bounce back from stress.

BOUNCING BACK FROM ANXIETY

Although stress and anxiety are often mentioned in the same sentence, it is important to notice the distinctions between the two. Stress is typically a reaction to external conditions—work, relationships, and social and community pressures. Anxiety is a person's specific reaction to stress, and its origin is internal (Ross, 2018). Anxiety is characterized by a persistent feeling of apprehension or dread in situations that are not actually threatening. Gripping fear and an immediate response, like jumping out of the way, is a completely rational response by a pedestrian crossing the street when an oncoming car is driven by someone who ignores the stoplight because he is looking at his phone. Anxiety, on the other hand, is the same gripping fear toward every car, even when it is stopped dead still. The same is true when anxiety is the response to every new colleague, new supervisor, new job, or new professional practice. The automatic response is fear and dread, sometimes to a paralyzing degree, rather than an inquiry into the reality of the situation. A specific manifestation of anxiety is post-traumatic stress disorder (PTSD) that arises due to traumatic events from the past. For the war veteran injured by an explosion, every loud noise can bring on a paralyzing response. For the adult who was the victim of child abuse, every attempt by another person to establish an intimate relationship can be threatening. Their anxiety is very real and rational when viewed in the context of their personal histories, but their response to this anxiety can impair their ability to lead a rich, full, and joyful life if they are not able to distinguish the past from the present. Symptoms of anxiety disorder include the following (Hurleuy, 2020):

- restlessness or feeling keyed up or on edge;
- difficulty controlling worry;
- easily fatigued;
- difficulty concentrating or mind going blank;
- irritability;
- muscle tension;
- sleep disturbance;
- exaggerated startle response;
- psychosomatic symptoms—headaches, stomachaches, dizziness, pins and needles;
- physical symptoms—shortness of breath, rapid heartbeat, excessive sweating, chest pain.

Certainly, some of these symptoms can occur to people

without a diagnosis of an anxiety disorder. But when anxiety becomes paralyzing, preventing a person from engaging in relationships and work, then it's time to seek professional help. Strategies to bounce back from anxiety involve physical, mental, and emotional resilience (Bowman, 2017).

Just as anxiety and stress affect us physically, some of the best ways to bounce back from anxiety include a physical regimen. Some people have found great relief through meditation and yoga. Please do not be put off by visions of balancing upside-down on one hand in a perfect pose. Yoga and meditation share in common an effort to remove distractions and a focus on breathing and the body, and these techniques are available to anyone with an open mind. Exercise need not be intimidating either, with everything from walks in the park to 20 minutes of intensive exercise offering benefits for mental health and cardio-vascular wellness in six weeks (Reynolds, 2017).

One of the best ways to bounce back from anxiety is to prevent its paralyzing effects before they occur. Taking regular breaks is an ideal way to interrupt the patterns that may provoke anxiety. While we are all subject to schedules—classes, meetings, and other demands—the evidence is clear that when we go for more than 90 minutes without a break, our cognitive powers decline. With regular breaks, research shows that people not only have better productivity but also exhibit better mental well-being and higher levels of creativity. Despite this evidence, however, most employees in the US rarely have a lunch break. Ask a teacher when was the last time they had lunch just to have a break rather than combining lunch with tutoring students, grading papers, or meeting with colleagues. Indeed, almost 40 percent of American workers felt that they were not encouraged to take breaks for lunch, and almost 20 percent reported that their supervisors would think that they are less productive if they took a lunch break. There is thus a deep irony in an administrator demanding that teachers give up their lunch time to listen to a presentation on evidence-based decision-making. The same is true for senior leadership teams who routinely work through lunch or perhaps serve food in order to have the illusion of multitasking. If we want to have engaged, focused, productive, and creative colleagues, they need to take real breaks. Interestingly, the trend toward working from home via online connections offered the promise of lower stress. You can work in your pajamas and walk the dog whenever you want! In reality, in widespread reports in the spring and summer of 2020, when working from home soared due to the closure of offices, schools, and other places of work during the COVID-19 pandemic, many workers reported spending more hours at work, fewer hours taking breaks or relaxing with family, and consequently higher levels of work-related stress and anxiety.

The third way in which people bounce back from anxiety is to breathe. Focusing on breath does not require a yoga or meditation class but can simply be 60 seconds of focused rhythmic breathing—in for four seconds, out for four seconds; in for five seconds, out for five seconds, and so on. To do this for only 60 seconds before a potentially stressful meeting, phone call, or other task can help create a sense of equanimity and calm that would never be present if you simply rush from one meeting to the next, from one call to the next, and from one task to the next. Breaks do not have to involve eating, walking, or exercise, though all of these activities are worthwhile. Do not underestimate the power of a breathing break for just one minute.

BOUNCING BACK FROM DEPRESSION

While stress and anxiety are often associated with specific events and causes, depression can be pervasive and long-lasting, often caused not by a specific event, but by chemical imbalances in the brain (Stephany, 2020). When I confessed a lack of understanding about brain chemistry and depression to a psychiatrist friend, she explained that it was not unlike wearing glasses. There's nothing that I did to cause far-sightedness, and there is nothing remarkable about wearing glasses to correct that condition. But, she said, we don't just "get over" eye conditions, and we should not expect to "get over" depression. It is a chronic and long-lasting condition that requires medical attention. Characterized by an overwhelming sense of listlessness, loneliness, and despair, depression can have effects ranging from occasional sadness to incapacitating paralysis. For some people, talk therapy, and in particular cognitive behavior therapy, has been shown to be an effective treatment for depression, while other patients require prescription medication (Clancy, 2020).

Resilience is an important part, but not the only part, of a comprehensive response to depression. Patients with symptoms of depression should first seek medical advice, as many conditions associated with depression may also affect major systems throughout the body. Moreover, if the depressed person is also abusing alcohol or drugs, then these conditions may require additional treatment. Therefore, the following ideas are suggestions for bouncing back from depression, but not for treating the illness itself. Bouncing back from depression falls into two separate categories: mental and physical. In a study of more than 2,500 adults with severe depression, 40 percent were able to recover fully and achieve what the researcher called complete mental health, compared to 78 percent of the non-depressed population, with a combination of regular physical exercise and a mental health regimen that included some involvement in spirituality (Fuller-Thompson et al., 2016). Other studies have reported significant levels of recovery from depression without spirituality but with a commitment to reframing the negative thoughts often associated with depression. Many studies of resilience from depression that I reviewed included physical exercise as a part of the recovery program. The National Institute of Mental Health estimates that of the 19 million Americans suffering from depression, over 80 percent benefit from treatment (WebMD, 2017). The striking difference between these two estimates of recovery may be explained by the American Psychiatric Institute study that suggests that even after recovery, about 50 percent of patients with major depression have one or more relapses.

With regard to psychological resilience, the research suggests we understand our red flags, the triggers that may instigate a depressive episode. These can include everything from a derisive comment or insult from a colleague or spouse to a seemingly innocuous suggestion. "You would really like my trainer!" becomes, "I'm fat and ugly and undesirable." Similarly, "This new time management system really works!" becomes "My boss thinks that I'm lazy and incompetent and can't manage my workload." In the language of cognitive behavioral therapy, this is catastrophizing; the key to resilience is an immediate reframing of our automatic thoughts to reality. The comment about the trainer is just that—a comment about the trainer and not about me. The comment about time management is about the system, not about me. It takes some deliberate effort, and many therapists suggest writing down the automatic thought that is full of catastrophic thinking, followed by a more accurate description of the conversation or event.

Bouncing back from depression is especially helped by the

consideration that depression is an illness and not a character flaw. When we attribute depressive thinking to a personal flaw, we equate it with immorality, cheating, and stealing. But if we broke a leg and missed a couple of days of work as a result, it would not occur to us to say, "I'm just lazy and worthless. Effective people don't break their legs." We don't blame ourselves for pneumonia, back injuries, or for that matter, COVID-19. These are unavoidable illnesses, and the medical evidence is clear that the brain chemistry associated with depression renders this an illness, not a deliberate choice (Marlow, 2017). It is also essential to recall that we would not simply "get over" a broken leg, pneumonia, appendicitis, or any other disease without professional help, and the evidence is substantial that psychotherapy, and in particular, cognitive behavioral therapy, is effective in treating depression.

Harvard Medical School Professor Dr. Michael Craig Miller notes that for most people, exercise works as well as antidepressants (Harvard Health Letter, 2019). Consistent low-intensity exercise not only improves mood but also has an observable impact on regions of the brain associated with improved mental health. While exercise fads come and go, Dr. Miller recommends that you select something that can be sustained over time. Many high-intensity routines, while good for cardiovascular health, go by the wayside with age and joint pain. An effective regimen related to brain health and designed to resist the symptoms of depression should be something you can envision using for the rest of your life.

While all treatment methods, including psychotherapy, pharmaceuticals, and exercise, may help people bounce back from depression, a comprehensive synthesis of randomized controlled trials (Blumenthal et al., 2012) suggests that exercise, for even as short a time as six weeks, has positive effects that are comparative to talk therapy and pharmaceutical treatments. Exercise has no side effects, no cost, and has additional benefits beyond treatment for depression.

Stress, anxiety, and depression are at the heart of the fear that afflicts individuals, schools, and entire systems. These conditions weaken our ability to respond to external threats and provide the care that students and colleagues require. Resilience in the face of stress, anxiety, and depression can seem like an overwhelming challenge. Indeed, in the helping professions, such as education, health care, and social work, dedicated people face the reality that time is a zero-sum game. In this equation, every hour devoted to the essential self-care required to bounce back from stress, anxiety, and depression is an hour that could have been devoted to caring for students, families, and patients. But this calculation is deeply flawed. In the absence of the resilience strategies described in this chapter, the result is not more time allocated to the care of those for whom we are responsible but more time allocated to preoccupation, fear, listlessness, and isolation. While not all educators and leaders are clinically depressed, I have never met one who is free from stress or anxiety. The best among them understands that measures taken for self-care—including time for gratitude, family, relationships, and exercise—are not deductions from time with students and colleagues but investments in their own health and resilience. By taking the time to build essential resilience, they will not eliminate stress, anxiety, and depression, but they certainly will create a bulwark of defenses from these psychological assaults. In sum, resilience is key to fearlessness. In the next chapter we will consider the keys to organizational resilience and apply the lessons of individual resilience to the entire school and educational system.

DISCUSSION QUESTIONS

1. Researchers cited in this chapter suggested that the first source of resilience in the face of stress is our mission. What is your mission, and how does it help you cope with stress? What differences do you find between your personal mission and that of your school or organization?

2. Reflections on personal experiences with loss and recovery can aid us in bouncing back from stress. Every reader has experienced the COVID-19 pandemic and its aftermath. Some readers recall the terrorist attacks of 9/11, the subsequent wars in Afghanistan and Iraq, and the pervasive fear accompanying those events. A few readers can recall the daily death tolls from the Vietnam War and the sense that this war would never end. How have your personal experiences with loss informed your ability to deal with stress?

3. Our locus of control significantly influences our psychological health. What are the factors that influence your health and happiness that, in your judgment, are clearly within your control right now?

4. Gratitude is a key to recovery from stress. What are three things for which you are most grateful right now?

5. Based on what you learned in the chapter, how would you distinguish among the causes and treatments for stress, anxiety, and depression?

CHAPTER 7.

ORGANIZATIONAL RESILIENCE

In this chapter—
- Anticipating Disruption
- Defining the Environment: The Unknown Unknowns
- Disciplined Decision-Making
- Discretion, Collaboration, and Centralization

D AVID DENYER REVIEWED MORE than 180 academic articles and a set of international case studies on organizational resilience. He defines the term as follows: "Organizational resilience is the ability of an organization to anticipate, prepare for, respond and adapt to incremental change and sudden disruptions in order to survive and prosper" (Denyer, 2017, p. 3). Resilience is essential for organizations that face challenges, especially challenges that threaten the survival of the organization and people within it. In seeking to become more resilient, organizations take two strikingly different paths: defensive, stopping bad things from happening; and progressive, making good things happen. In the early stages of a crisis, organizations trend to be defensive: They stay inside during the threat of virus, focus on learning the fundamentals of reading and math for underperforming schools, police the streets in high-crime areas. These are all rational reactions to current threats. But when systems are stuck in this mode of defensive thinking, they rely on monitoring and compliance, tactics that eventually demoralize people within the organization and those they wish to serve. To break out of a compliance-dependent system, organizations must be sufficiently adaptive and flexible to innovate solutions that are lasting. The research on organizational thinking suggests that leaders engage in paradoxical thinking—that is, "balancing preventative control, mindful action, performance optimization and adaptive innovation, and managing the tensions inherent in these distance perspectives" (Denyer, 2017, p. 8). In the context of educational systems, this requires that schools not only embrace technology but also maintain one-to-one relationships between students and teachers with and without new technologies. Lessons from the COVID-19 pandemic suggest that interpersonal contacts through old-fashioned telephones, sidewalk visits, and other personal connections—all at a safe distance—are better than the illusion that mere placement of a computer in the hands of a child guarantees connection, engagement, and learning. In this chapter we will explore how resilient schools anticipate disruptions. This extends far beyond the traditional drills for fires and tornadoes and includes a wide range of scenario planning. Next, we will consider defining the environment with a candid acknowledgment of what we know and what remains unknown. While leadership decision-making is never perfect, it can be improved with discipline and an understanding that uncertainty and luck, as well as good strategy, influence every outcome. Finally, we will consider the types of decisions made in every educational system, from groups of teachers to large and complex systems. Some decisions are discretionary, some require collaboration, and others depend upon centralized authority.

The tough part is deciding which decisions fit best with which level of decision-making, and then communicating that clearly throughout the organization

ANTICIPATING DISRUPTION

While few people anticipated the exceptional educational and economic disruptions associated with the COVID-19 pandemic, some educational systems did anticipate the need for distance learning and technology access for all students. Well before the pandemic led to widespread school closings and the need for distance learning, technology advocates noted that internet connectivity was the key to equity (Anderson, 2019). But when the COVID pandemic hit, the reality was far short of the promise. Approximately 14 percent of school-age children, or about 9.4 million students, were without internet connections. The picture in historically disadvantaged families was far worse. While 12 percent of white and Asian children lacked internet access in 2020, 37 percent of Native Nation and Alaska Native children were without internet, 19 percent of black children and 17 percent of Hispanic children could not connect to school for their virtual lessons (Camera, 2020). Many of these students were already behind in fundamental reading and math skills, and without access to instruction they fell farther behind their more advanced peers. While there are examples of heroic efforts by teachers to reach every student, the reality is that individual heroism is not a sustainable strategy for schools. Educational systems cannot rely on superhuman efforts that burn out teachers and administrators.

In the 1950s, children learned to "duck and cover," with the presumption that hiding beneath a pressed-wood desktop would protect them from nuclear blasts (Grieve, 2018). Many readers recall fire drills in which children walked in an orderly fashion outside of the building while invisible flames raged within—and tornado drills, in which they stood silently within interior walls, safely away from the shattering glass of classroom windows. In more recent years, children have learned to comply with active shooter drills with strategies varying widely in their efficacy. Many of these drills have been determined to range from unproven to actively detrimental to student safety (Walker, 2020). The biggest impact on school safety and operations was the 2020 COVID-19 pandemic, yet I am not aware of any pandemic drills or even serious planning for massive school closures. The reflexive decisions throughout the nation to close schools failed to consider the evidence that in many cases, students' basic needs for food, safety, and learning were better met in school than when they were barred from school grounds. For the one in seven children in the US facing food insecurity, they are more likely to receive consistent and nutritious meals at school than at home (Feeding America, 2020). In many cases, students are also safer in school than at home (Sherfinski, 2018). In school, students learn the warning signs of potential violence, are surrounded by caring adults who love them and care about them, and most importantly, are kept safe from the violence that too often awaits them on the streets or even at home. Moreover, parents—especially working single parents struggling to make ends meet—cannot drop their job obligations and stay home. Leaving young children at home, sometimes under the supervision of other children, is a recipe for danger and unnecessary risk. Perhaps the greatest long-term cost of shutting students out of school is the enduring decline in literacy skills that will inevitably increase the dropout rate and its accompanying costs of unemployment, poverty, greater medical needs, and increased involvement in the criminal justice system (Alliance for Excellent

Education, 2015). When making the decision to close schools, decision-makers considered a false comparison—the danger of the COVID-19 virus to a mythically pure and safe environment outside of school. This was a classic failure of systems thinking, in which leaders must recognize that changes in one part of every system inevitably influence other parts of the system. It remains to be seen how student morbidity and mortality was influenced as a result of school closures. Unfortunately, if policymakers refuse to even consider the question and conduct the research, then we will never know how to make better decisions in the future.

What are other events educational leaders should anticipate? Here are five disruptions leaders should contemplate for the years 2021 through 2030:

1. Work Stoppages. Large numbers of staff members refuse to come to schools and other buildings that they regard as unsafe. With approximately 29 percent of teacher ranks over the age of 50, schools could face not only a dire shortage of teachers, but age discrimination complaints as well if districts attempted to take adverse actions against teachers who refuse to work in schools.

2. Financial Distress. Revenues from local property taxes, state sales taxes, and state income taxes, on which many school districts depend, could decline drastically. The likelihood of local voters to approve bond issues and tax hikes will be negligible. At the same time, retirement funds that have guaranteed to provide employees from school systems an income for life have seen their value plummet by more than 30 percent. Without sufficient capital to pay retirement benefits and without the robust returns on investments that these funds have been experiencing in the past several years, districts will see mandatory payments to retirement funds increase while revenues are declining. Harvard economics professor and former Secretary of the Treasure Lawrence Summers summarized the human and economic impact of the COVID-19 pandemic as follows:

> This crisis is a massive global event in terms of its impact. Take an American perspective. Almost certainly more Americans will die of COVID-19 than have died in all the military conflicts of the past 70 years. Some respectable projections suggest that more may die than in all the wars of the 20th century. This spring's job losses have come at a far faster rate than at any point in history, and many forecasters believe that unemployment will be above its post-Depression high for two years. (Summers, 2020)

The impact on school budgets will start with the big-ticket items; construction and remodeling plans will be cancelled, even when construction and remodeling might save costs compared to the essential maintenance on aging buildings. After that, administrative ranks will be the easiest targets for personnel costs, and districts that are accustomed to having a set of assistant superintendents, executive directors, and directors will be left with a skeleton crew focused more on compliance than on instructional leadership. Class sizes will expand from their already high levels. Some California schools I visited in 2019 and early 2020 already had nearly forty students in a classroom designed for thirty, with no room for group meetings or movement.

3. Teacher Shortages. Even with jobs in short supply, expect teachers to leave the profession and fewer people to enter the pipeline of teacher preparation. The research clearly indicates that the teacher shortage is not caused by low wages alone but also by poor working conditions, a factor destined to become worse in the years ahead (D. Reeves, 2018). Students in teacher preparation programs in the spring of 2020 were unable to participate in traditional student teaching programs and thus will arrive in classrooms completely unprepared for the challenges of classroom management and the routine tasks of the daily life of teaching. Leadership should not be surprised by burnout and departures of teachers early in their career. They will be replaced by people who have emergency credentials and are without the background and training to understand and deliver curriculum, manage a classroom, or assess student learning.

4. Competition from Private Online Education Providers. Expect a new generation of charter schools and private schools to offer communities bargain-basement pricing for schools, an appealing opportunity for cash-strapped states. Previously established caps on charter schools and institutional resistance to private schools may wither away if policymakers believe that they can save money (Kent, 2020). K–12, Inc. and other online providers are already delivering services to more than 375,000 students, and their digital platforms allow for rapid expansion. Abandoned theaters and shopping malls are going to provide low-cost facilities for charters and other alternative providers. More than two million students are already homeschooled, and surveys suggest more than 13 percent of parents would like to homeschool their children. Expect some small districts, already threatened with takeovers and consolidations by their larger neighbors, to convert entirely to remote learning, reserving the old school buildings for community events. As larger districts face additional revenue losses from this new competition, expect them to create options including in-district charter schools and virtual schools. In May 2020, the U.S. Department of Education announced that they would divert funding intended for public schools to private schools, including religious schools and home-school families, and would require local public-school districts to share federal funds with local private schools (Green, 2020). This is despite the revenue losses from decreasing state and local tax revenues that will cause significant layoffs and other cost-cutting measures for the 2020–2021 school year and beyond.

5. Pre–K to 16 Consolidation. Federal and state funds remain available for preschool, so expect more districts to offer early childhood education. In addition, as traditional college models fail due to high costs and inadequate enrollment (Busteed, 2019), expect innovative educational systems that traditionally served the K–12 market to expand their services at both ends, including child care at a very early age and postsecondary education for associates, bachelors, and higher degrees.

While none of these five disruptions is particularly surprising, the most perplexing thing will be school leaders who are caught unawares as their revenues decline, their competition increases, and their labor force is in a shambles. Leaders must, therefore, take immediate steps to define their current and future environments.

DEFINING THE ENVIRONMENT: THE UNKNOWN UNKNOWNS

During the early stages of the wars in Afghanistan and Iraq, Secretary of Defense Donald Rumsfeld famously described the challenges of information available to policymakers. At a February 12, 2002 news briefing, he explained:

> There are known knowns. There are things we know we know. We also know there are known unknowns. That is to say, we know there are some things we do not know. But there are also unknown unknowns, the ones we don't know we don't know. (Shermer, 2005)

Although comedians have enjoyed a couple of decades of ridicule at Rumsfeld's expense, the truth is that he was right. And despite the inelegant way Rumsfeld expressed it, educational leaders must parse out the information they have and identify the uncertainties before them as well as the information they need. That is, they must know the known knowns, taking care to gather all the relevant information they have. This includes a serious commitment to systems thinking—an understanding of how one part of the system influences every other part. For example, we cannot consider the risks of students being in school without balancing the risks of students not being in school. Next, leaders must identify the known unknowns and conduct a vigorous information-gathering campaign. For example, we may not know how many students lack technology access, but with a comprehensive needs assessment, we can address that known unknown. We may not know how many children and staff members have been vaccinated against a variety of diseases, but that is information we can gather. The most challenging part of defining the environment for leaders is the set of unknown unknowns. We can't gather information for areas we do not even know about. In January of 2020, almost no one was gathering information on COVID-19 infections and deaths. Three months later, this was the stuff of daily reports from federal, state, and local officials. Let us consider some possible unknown unknowns. While by definition we do not know the questions to be addressed, we can consider various categories of interest to educational leaders. These include, for example,

Staff. We know their age, gender, and health history, at least in terms of sick days reported. Can we develop a model that estimates the impact of a second wave of COVID-19 or other pandemics on the staff in terms of days off, additional medical care costs (especially for districts that have self-funded health insurance systems), and disruptions to particular specialties, such as special education?

Funding. We already have estimates of revenues from state and local resources. Can we also develop models of other impacts on school funding, including migration of students to private schools, other districts, and homeschool? Can we estimate the impact on school funding of increasingly obsolete facilities that are not updated or improved due to the probable failure of bond issues? What is the impact if the district declares bankruptcy?

Organization and Structure. Can we generate alternative scenarios in which the district becomes engaged in more extensive early childhood education, postsecondary education, mergers with other districts, and mergers with colleges or universities? What is the impact if the district eliminates one or more layers of administration at the central office and building levels? What is the impact of school consolidation, with one principal responsible for two or more schools?

This sort of scenario planning can be deeply uncomfortable, as this morning's scenario can become this afternoon's rampant rumor. Leaders are therefore faced with the awkward choice of failing to engage in consideration of the unknown unknowns and are later accused of insufficient preparation for the next crisis, or they face criticism for considering scenarios that seem wild and outrageous based on the information currently available. We are today indebted to Thomas Hobson, a livery owner in Cambridge, England, in the 16th century for the idiom "Hobson's choice," in which one must make a "take it or leave it" decision (Merriam-Webster Dictionary, n.d.). Leaders faced with the Hobson's choice of today will have a consensus recommendation from their staff and then take it or leave it. In the next section, we will consider why this is a terrible idea and how, especially in times of crisis and high risk, leaders must engage in disciplined decision-making.

DISCIPLINED DECISION-MAKING

People are typically uncomfortable with conflict. This starts early in school, when students learn that the price of criticism can be social isolation. As I heard a middle school student, Maddy, explain, "I knew that my friend Terrance made a mistake in his essay, but I didn't tell him because it might have hurt his feelings." Thus, Terrance did not benefit from feedback that might have improved his writing, and Maddy's fear of conflict was reinforced. But fast forward a few decades, and Maddy is now the superintendent of schools. She loves and cares about her colleagues and doesn't want to hurt their feelings. The culture of the leadership team prizes consensus over conflict, and the staff knows that the safest thing to do when major decisions come up is to hash out the alternatives and then take a recommendation to the superintendent. They provide a Hobson's choice—take it or leave it—option to the leader.

There is a better way, and that is mutually exclusive decision alternatives. Most leaders have learned the hard way that staff members who seek to avoid conflict offer them a Hobson's choice. An infamous example of this faulty decision-making process was the 1962 Bay of Pigs fiasco, the ill-fated invasion of Cuba by underequipped and outmanned operatives supported by the CIA. Many were slaughtered on the beach, and the rest were imprisoned by the Castro regime. Five days after the failed invasion, President Kennedy met with his predecessor, Dwight Eisenhower. In their secret talks at Camp David, Eisenhower asked about the decision-making process involved in the invasion, and President Kennedy replied that the CIA, Joint Chiefs of Staff, and State Department had agreed and given him only one decision option (Gellman, 2015). Later, in 1963, with the stakes immeasurably higher, President Kennedy faced the Cuban Missile Crisis, where Soviet nuclear missiles capable of striking the US in a matter of minutes were being installed in Cuba, only 90 miles from U.S. land. But during days of decisions and negotiations that brought the world back from the brink of nuclear conflict, Kennedy encouraged open conflict and debate among his advisors.

> He [Kennedy] removed the protocols and hierarchies that normally affect communication and allowed his team to discuss options as peers. He asked hard questions, removed himself from some of the discussions so as not to affect the outcome of the conversations, and allowed differing ideas and viewpoints to be fully fleshed out and considered. (Mullane, 2017)

Because so many staff members and senior executives rise to their positions by carefully avoiding conflict and exercising the political skills necessary to build consensus, conflict is uncomfortable. This creates a culture of winners and losers, and nobody likes to lose, especially if they have devoted decades of their careers to rising through the ranks with little or no conflict. Therefore, like President Kennedy when he faced the greatest crisis of his brief presidency, leaders must not only allow for the emergence of conflicting ideas but also actively encourage it. Leadership scholars have, in the decades since the Cuban Missile Crisis, considered their illusion of rigor in which experts and staff members converge around a single solution rather than engage in the vigorous debate essential to effective decisions. Strategic planning exercises in particular consume enormous amounts of time and yet have little to show for it. In a seminal article on this subject in the *Harvard Business Review*, "Bringing Science to the Art of Strategy," the authors made a compelling argument for mutually exclusive decision alternatives (Lafley et al., 2012, September). Leaders may find it necessary to assign staff members to identify a particular alternative, to present the advantages and disadvantages of it, and to argue for the disadvantages of other alternatives advocated by colleagues. This shifts the culture from winning or losing a particular policy choice to a culture of improving the decision-making process. To gain access to the leadership table requires the intellectual rigor and personal non-defensiveness to engage in the give-and-take of policy debate without personal antagonism or hurt feelings. Consider your own experience with bad decisions, especially in people, money, and technology. Many bad decisions can be traced to a take-it-or-leave-it choice, where the staff appeared to be in unanimous agreement, and the leader only had to bless that choice. In fact, there were disagreements, but those disagreements took place out of earshot of the leader, denying the leader and the organization the opportunity to learn from those debates.

DISCRETION, COLLABORATION, AND CENTRALIZATION

There are three types of decisions in most educational systems: discretionary, collaborative, or centralized. Discretionary decisions occur without approval; they are simply the minute-to-minute decisions made by teachers and other staff members about how to do the work at hand. In the classroom, this happens with the way students are grouped and regrouped, how teachers respond in the moment to the individual needs of students, and many other areas of professional discretion. In the superintendent's office, discretionary decisions might include setting the agenda for cabinet meetings and how to communicate on important items to the board and community stakeholders.

Collaborative decisions require working with colleagues to come to a consensus. For example, when teachers are operating in the context of a professional learning community, they are obliged to create common formative assessments so that the same student in the same grade level in the same subject is assessed in the same way (DuFour et al., 2006). They are also required to engage in collaborative scoring so that teachers agree on what the word "proficient" means when they look at examples of student work (D. Reeves, 2020a). Similarly, it is very helpful when governing board leaders and senior administrative team members collaborate on how to communicate key ideas to parents and students.

Centralized decisions are made by a higher authority and must be carried out by teachers and administrators. For example, state and provincial authorities typically establish academic standards, and it is up to educators and administrators to ensure that the knowledge and skills in those standards are provided to students. State and national bodies establish financial accounting standards, and local districts are obliged to keep the books according to those rules.

When I surveyed teachers about these three types of decisions, they were consistent in their views that almost three-quarters of decisions were centralized, representing top-down authority from external decision-makers, and thought that only 4 percent of decisions were discretionary. But when I analyzed actual decisions made in the classroom, a different picture emerged; only 27 percent of decisions were the result of top-down authority and the remainder was divided between collaborative decisions and those made on a discretionary basis by teachers (D. B. Reeves, 2021). When I interviewed teachers to try to better understand the difference between the perception and reality of decision-making structures, I learned that teachers were willing to accept an appreciable degree of external authority. Said one, "We don't need to vote on fire drills." But they were driven to distraction about the ambiguity of the process. They thought some decisions were mandatory and discovered only late in the school year that they had discretion. Conversely, they had been led to believe that some curriculum and assessment decisions were discretionary, only to discover later that either collaboration was required with other teachers or that the district had already made system-level decisions on curriculum, instructional methods, and classroom assessment. The lesson from these pervasive misunderstandings is that leaders must be clear about which decisions are associated with which levels—discretionary, collaborative, and centralized.

Some general guidance for decision-making might be the following: If it is a matter of safety and values, centralized decision-making is required. For a system committed to equity, for example, inequitable decisions are not permitted, no matter how strong the opinions of the individual teacher nor how clear the consensus is by a collaborative team. These misunderstandings are especially common when the issue is the grading policies of individual teachers. My research with more than 10,000 teachers and administrators reveals that the same student with the identical performance can receive grades from A to F based not on differences in performance, but based entirely on the idiosyncratic grading practices of the individual teacher (D. B. Reeves, 2016). If equity is a value in your school or system, it is simply not acceptable to have grades for identical student work vary from A to F, as that would indicate that factors other than actual student performance are used to determine the grade. Similarly, if there is a clear system or school disciplinary policy that requires that behavior such as incomplete work, disrespect, eye-rolling, or head on the desk is to be addressed in the classroom by the teacher, then it is a prescription for inequity for some students to be sent to the office for this behavior and other students to have the same behavior addressed in class without an office referral. These inconsistencies take on especially grave consequences when districts have rules such as three office referrals leading to an automatic suspension. What begins as a minor inequity becomes a major source of disproportional treatment of students. Moreover, one suspension after another quickly leads to failure in multiple courses, and multiple failures leads to dropouts with a lifetime of consequences for health, crime, and unemployment (Alliance for Excellent Education, 2015). The same requirements for equity apply to relationships between administrators and teachers. When some teachers receive negative evaluations for insufficient engagement with students and too much direct presentation of information, yet other teachers do the same thing and their practices are tolerated, then this too violates the value of equity. In sum, values are not discretionary; if they were, they would not be values but only personal preferences.

Similarly, the definition of collaborative decision-making varies widely from one school to the next and even within schools. Collaborative teams in the context of schools require teacher consensus on what students are expected to learn and how that learning will be assessed. If there are, for example, common academic standards but different methods of assessing student learning and different levels of performance that are regarded as proficient, the collaboration has no meaning. These groups of teachers are not engaged in professional learning communities (PLCs), but only in "PLC Lite" (DuFour & Reeves, 2016). If fairness is a fundamental value, and collaborative assessment and scoring is the way a school is pursuing that value, then wide variations in assessment and expectations are violations of the value of fairness. While no school or educational system can endure in an environment of micromanagement, essential values cannot be meaningful when leaders abdicate every decision on curriculum, assessment, and discipline to the idiosyncratic judgments that vary from one classroom to another, one hallway to another, and one school to another.

In this chapter we considered how to anticipate disruption. While no leader has a crystal ball, it is certainly possible to consider variations in the internal and external factors that influence educational success. Defining the environment requires scenario planning, including an attempt to consider the unknown unknowns—the conditions that we do not know, do not anticipate, and are by definition surprising and unexpected. Nevertheless, we can practice scenario planning to develop the skills of systems thinking among leaders and staff. History teaches us the folly of Hobson's choice, the take-it-or-leave-it illusion of consensus that most leaders confront. Far better to embrace the value of debate—clearly articulated decision alternatives. Even if it is necessary to assign staff members to defend or attack positions that are at odds with their personal viewpoints, the health of the system's decision-making process is best served by a disciplined set of alternatives, each with clearly outlined advantages and disadvantages. Finally, leaders must consider three types of decisions: discretionary, collaborative, and centralized. The key to effective leadership communication is to link carefully each decision to its decision type. Leaders can say, "Here is the outline of results we need, and you have the discretion to choose how to achieve these results" for discretionary decisions. Or they can say, "While you have some discretion, you must collaborate with your colleagues in order to provide fair and consistent treatment of students." Or they can say, "Colleagues, this is a matter of our values, so I am not asking for a vote. We will execute this decision in this way." While centralized decisions cannot be employed for every decision, it is vital to provide clarity to all stakeholders about which decisions are centralized, which are collaborative, and which are discretionary. In Part III, we will consider fearlessness in practice, and how classrooms, schools, and systems will provide the safe, challenging, and engaging environments that our students and colleagues deserve.

DISCUSSION QUESTIONS

1. One key to organizational resilience is anticipating disruption. What disruptions can you anticipate in the next three months? For the next year? In three, five, and ten years?

2. As you seek to define the challenges ahead, what are the
   • known knowns—the facts you have in hand;
   • known unknowns—the questions you need to answer;
   • unknown unknowns—the areas in which you may not yet know the question to ask.

3. Think of a decision that you or your leadership team must make in the weeks or months ahead. Think especially of high-impact decisions such as those involving people, money, or technology. Once you have identified the most important of these decisions, think of at least two alternative decisions. There is no compromise—you or the leadership team must choose one decision or the other. What are the advantages and disadvantages of each alternative? Did this exercise help any new decision alternatives or considerations to emerge that might be of help in making the final decision?

4. This chapter considered three types of decisions: discretionary, collaborative, or centralized. Considering only your personal perspective based on your current professional responsibility, what is an example of each type of decision? Which decision areas are unclear—that is, it's not certain whether a decision is discretionary, collaborative, or centralized? How can you resolve that ambiguity?

PART III:

FEARLESSNESS IN PRACTICE

I T IS EASY TO be fearless in theory. That is why critics of the educational system prefer the safety of armchair rebukes to the real-world challenges of the classroom, hallways, or principal's office of real schools. In Chapter 8 we will consider the teacher's perspective of the fearless classroom and the fundamental need to trust oneself and one's colleagues. In Chapter 9 we will consider the challenge of fearless leadership. Fearlessness in this context does not imply recklessness; rather, it ensures the presence, communication, and personal responsibility that has nothing to do with physical prowess and everything to do with leadership character. In Chapter 10 we will consider fearless change, the very essence of what fearlessness is all about. Fearful leaders hide behind the comfortable present and are unable to forge the way ahead to the unknown. Interestingly, part of leading change is also being clear and reassuring about what does not change. Leaders who change nothing are cowards. Leaders who change everything are fools. Finally, in Chapter 11 we will consider the essential nature of fearless systems, exploring the systems thinking that is the hallmark of every person in a fearless organization.

CHAPTER 8

FEARLESS CLASSROOMS

In this chapter—

- Fearless Learning
- Trust in the Teacher
- Trust in Peers
- Trust in Self

F ROM A VERY EARLY age, students are conditioned to seek the right answer. That's not a problem when the question concerns the sum of two plus two. But it is deeply problematic when the question is, "How are you feeling?" Students yearn to give the right answer, an impulse that can obscure effective and essential communication with teachers and peers. In this chapter we will explore the components of the fearless classroom. First, we will consider the elements of fearless learning, which include not only the freedom to make mistakes but also the creation of a safe environment in which to learn from these mistakes. Then we will consider how teachers create trust by transforming the role of students from pleasers— trying to make every adult in their lives happy—to colearners. Perhaps the most challenging element of the fearless classroom is building trust in peers. Although we love videos of the joyful squeals of the happy classroom, teachers and parents also know that kids can be pretty darn mean sometimes, placing vulnerable classmates on edge and causing them to fear expressing anything less than conformity with the crowd. Fortunately, there are evidence-based practices to build kindness, empathy, and trust among students. Finally, we will consider how to help students build trust in themselves, confidently expressing pride, doubt, fears, and mistakes.

FEARLESS LEARNING

The key to fearless learning is a classroom environment characterized by inquiry, discovery, trial and error—many, many errors—and at last, the sublime sense of accomplishment that comes from a breakthrough. Fearful learning is knowing that the failure to answer a question from the teacher will lead to giggles, catcalls, and a disappointed look from the teacher. Fearless learning is knowing that the path of discovery requires jumping in the lake of uncertainty and searching for understanding, confident that friends and teachers are there to help you on the journey. Fearful learning is characterized by all-or-nothing thinking—either you are a genius or a fool, a good student or one who disappoints the adults in your life. Fearless learning is not characterized by confidence in always providing the right answer; rather, its hallmark is in always knowing that the joy of school lies not merely in recitation of memorized facts, but in the endlessly fascinating pursuit of understanding. Fearful learning is knowing that insects have six legs and being prepared to provide that answer at a moment's notice. Fearless learning is wondering aloud why some bugs have six legs and others, like spiders, have eight legs. How did that happen? And the key to fearless learning is when the teacher says, "I don't know—let's find out together."

Fearless learning requires an environment of trust and confidence as well as models of what fearless learning looks like in people who students and teachers admire. Instead of putting heroes on the pedestal of perfection, students learn wonderful lessons when they understand that Einstein made plenty of mistakes on the road to relativity, that George Washington lost more battles than he won, that Beethoven wrote some truly awful music, and that DaVinci and most other artists discarded far more pieces of art than are displayed in museums. They learn not only from the leadership and inspirational speeches of leaders of the Civil Rights movement but also from their mistakes. While it is not necessary to deconstruct our heroes, it is essential that we see them as humans with insights and actions that guide us, instead of as superhumans who are beyond our reach. The students of the 21st century will follow space exploration to the moon, Mars, and beyond, and they are almost certain to witness failures along the way (Varol, 2020). These events, which will transfix the attention of students around the globe as surely as the first earth orbit and first footsteps on the moon did in an earlier generation, provide an ideal opportunity for classrooms to think not only of the expertise and heroism of astronauts but of how even the best and brightest people and organizations make mistakes and learn from them as well.

An understanding of fearless learning also requires a quest for clarity rather than complexity. As students progress through the grades, they can easily equate rhetorical flourish with knowledge. Thus, it is immensely helpful that they know that leaders, thinkers, and discoverers prize simplicity over obscurity and elevate shorter words over longer ones (Gallo, 2020). Today's students will have endured and survived a global pandemic and economic crisis, and the classroom may be the only fearless environment in their lives. They depend on their classroom for honesty, candor, and safety.

TRUST IN THE TEACHER

Teachers are the beacons of trust in fearless schools. Students know that they can confide in teachers, telling them about their hopes and fears, ambitions and doubts. Teachers know that as important as their language is ("I'm so proud of you!"), their nonverbal cues can be read in an instant by students. The furrowed brow, raised eyebrows, and unintentional but very real looks of disappointment can be as crushing as any words the teacher may utter. Even well-intentioned techniques such as "phone a friend," in which students are encouraged to ask a peer for help when they don't know the answer, signals to the student that when they are struggling, the immediate response of the teacher is not persistence, struggle, resilience, and discovery—but a default to a peer who enjoys the teacher's approval.

Special educators are often models of brilliant persistence. When a student with a learning disability struggles with an unfamiliar word or challenging problem, the response is rarely to admit defeat and ask a peer or adult for help. Rather, they will take a task and break it down into smaller incremental tasks. What I, as a math teacher, think is a single problem, my special education colleague will help me to understand is four discrete steps. These insights make me a better teacher and makes my students more confident and fearless as they approach previously inscrutable problems.

Fearless teachers are vulnerable, frequently acknowledging what they are learning and how much they enjoy learning new things they didn't know before. In contrast to the teacher whose personal and professional identity is dependent upon displays of expertise, the fearless teacher acknowledges "I'm stumped" and follows it up with "Let's work on this together." The transformation from unchallenged expertise and dominance to codiscovery requires an exceptionally secure ego and professional confidence. Secondary teachers will put up with the wisecracks of "You're supposed to be the teacher and you're supposed to give us the answers." They know that they do not serve the intellectual and emotional development of students by being a human Google search engine; rather, they choose to accomplish this by challenging students, engaging them in the process of discovery, and resisting the temptation to ease the discomfort of ignorance. Teachers are not, in brief, order-takers who are there to satisfy the demands of the customer. When students assume the role of customer, they are paralyzed without the clerk, cook, and wait-staff to cater to their needs. Without this bevy of adults to serve them, students are fearful. When adults are literally and figuratively on the same side of the classroom, students become fearless, joining teachers on the voyage of discovery.

As important as fearless teaching is in the classroom, it is equally important in the context of collaboration with professional colleagues. Although schools around the world often claim to have PLCs, there are widely varying degrees to which the principles of PLCs are applied (DuFour & Reeves, 2016). The same meeting label with the same time allocation supported by the same professional learning can take two widely divergent paths. One path is genuine collaboration, in which teachers share learning goals, common assessments, interventions for students in need, and learning extensions where appropriate. Teachers in these collaborative meetings share not only their most effective practices but also their mistakes, and they eagerly learn from their colleagues. They examine data analysis for the entire grade and review case studies of students who are making great strides in learning. Other collaborative meetings claim to follow the tenets of PLCs, but they are little more than data displays. They are looking at data in the same manner in which they might look at animals in the zoo—it's interesting, but they gain little insight from mere observation. The teachers and administrators in these ineffective meetings are smart and professional, so what prevents them from the essential productive conversations about student learning and professional practices? In a word, fear. They fear embarrassment and judgment. Teachers tell me that discussing student data on a class-by-class basis feels evaluative and that comparisons of one teacher to another are inevitable. "Better to remain silent," they reason, "than to have my administrators and peers think I am incompetent."

Effective leaders, including building administrators, instructional coaches, and PLC team leaders, have an obligation to place relentless focus on a fearless environment. Just as effective teachers do in the classroom, the leaders in effective collaborative teams focus on discovery, not on the right answer. They enthusiastically value candid discussions of mistakes and how teachers recognize, learn from, and recover from errors. Their perspective when looking at data and individual pieces of student work is the treasure hunt, not the witch hunt. It is thrilling to see effective leaders transform a demoralized group of teachers into confident heroes as the leader digs well beneath the average test scores, charts, and statistics, and finds cases of extraordinary student improvement. This practice, which requires considerable persistence on the part of leaders, changes defensiveness into pride in a matter of moments. These leaders know that we will not have fearless classrooms without fearless collaborative team meetings. In sum, a great PLC is a fearless PLC.

TRUST IN PEERS

Students can be wonderfully decent, caring, and kind. Friendships, from preschool though adulthood, are the lifeline that humans need for emotional survival. Indeed, the need for interpersonal connection is adaptive from our most ancient ancestors. Exclusion from the tribe meant certain death on the Serengeti, and inclusion led to access to food, shelter, and safety. The visceral need to be part of the tribe is equally real today (Junger, 2016). Children unacquainted with anthropological research have a deep understanding of tribes, as exclusion from the lunch table, game, or discussion group is as painful as exclusion from the group of our Homo sapiens ancestors.

Sometimes exclusions are malicious, perhaps in retaliation for some perceived slight or retribution for showing off. As the Australians say, the tallest poppies are the first to get chopped off. But other times the exclusion is well-intentioned but equally harmful. You'll recall the middle schooler, Maddy, whom we met in Chapter 7, and her reluctance to tell her friend Terrance about the errors in his essay because she was afraid to hurt his feelings. Maddy thought she was being nice, but her distrust of how Terrance might react to her assistance and feedback prevented her from being a good friend and withheld from Terrance the feedback he needed to become a better writer.

Building trust in peers requires effort and intentionality by the teacher and by student leaders. Some teachers wisely use daily classroom meetings so that students can check in with one another and, most essentially, learn their names and personal interests. Trust in peers also requires careful structuring of group work and discussions so that all students have an important role to play and do not depend upon a few peers to carry the load. The premium in these discussions is not on knowing the right answers, but on asking questions and bringing to the group both knowledge and prompts for discovery (Bouchard, 2019).

TRUST IN SELF

Students may trust their teachers, peers, parents, and even strangers. But sometimes the greatest challenge to trust and the fearlessness that follows is to trust themselves. When students believe in themselves and maintain a hopeful outlook on their ability to influence their future, they not only do better academically but are also less susceptible to stress, anxiety, and depression (Zakrzewski, 2017). The key to trusting oneself is not the illusion of perfection and always having the right answer; rather, it is the confidence that making mistakes is the path to success (Eva, 2017). Fearless students are not perfect and do not pursue that fantasy. They understand the difference between learning mistakes—hypotheses about the world that turned out not to be valid—and careless mistakes. This commitment to trial and error begins in the crib, as babies are natural hypothesis testers, as Stanford psychologist Allison Gopnik (2016) has demonstrated. If babies didn't use trial and error as a regular part of their toddler mindset, they would never learn to walk or talk.

So what happened between the fearless children who, after crashing and falling innumerable times on the path to becoming proficient walkers, became timid and fearful students in class? Consider the environment surrounding those first steps. From the sounds of the crowd, that toddler just won the Super Bowl, World Cup, and intergalactic chess championship all in a single moment. All the falls and missteps were ancient history, with every important person in the life of that child focused on the ultimate victory. In just a few short years, however, the thrill of victory is replaced by the humiliation of defeat. A perfect story is marred by a mispronounced word, as parents, teachers, siblings, and peers are focused on correction rather than celebration. The perfect math papers adorn the bulletin board and refrigerator door, while the mistakes are in the trash. Emotional losses receive similarly disproportionate weight, as a single unkind word replaces a roomful of friendships. As Tierney and Baumeister (2019) explain in *The Power of Bad,* negative events and comments are far more enduring than positive ones, and what the researchers call the negative effect has profound and lasting impact for children and adults.

Helping students build trust in themselves requires relearning the lessons of infancy. Not only do children striving to walk and talk make many mistakes but they also get accurate feedback, if not always from their parents, at least from the floor, wall, and lamps into which they bump on their way to success. These obstacles are the opposite of the false self-esteem that children sometimes hear, the inaccurate message that they achieved something that they know they did not achieve. The cheers were for real steps, and the love and encouragement were associated with real falls. Infants receive accurate and continuous feedback, a vital source of information that becomes elusive as they enter school. With each passing year, students are as likely to be rewarded for sullen compliance as for proficiency, and thus an astounding number of students in middle and high school receive honor roll grades without a hint of proficiency (D. Reeves, 2020a). If we want to help students trust themselves, they must trust the adults in their lives at school as much as they trusted when they were learning to walk.

In this chapter we considered the creation and maintenance of the fearless classroom. We learned that a fearless learning environment is based on trust in teachers, peers, and oneself. In the next chapter we will turn our attention to fearless leadership—the essential ingredient for fearless schools.

DISCUSSION QUESTIONS

1. Learning, by definition, requires the replacement of previous knowledge with new knowledge. Think of a time when you learned something new and challenging. What previous ideas did you need to discard in order to accept the new learning?

2. Reflect on your experience as a student, either in K–12 education or as an adult. How did teachers encourage you to take risks and learn? What were the ways—obvious and subtle—that teachers discouraged risk-taking, discovery, and learning?

3. When you were a student, how did your peers encourage and discourage learning? Today, as a professional, how do peers encourage and discourage learning?

4. Fearless learning requires trust in oneself. Think of a situation in which you overcame doubt, trusted yourself, took a risk, and learned something important. How does that experience inform your learning today?

CHAPTER 9.

FEARLESS LEADERSHIP

In this chapter—
- The Central Message: What Does *Not* Change
- Fearless Presence
- Fearless Communication
- Fearless Decision-Making
- Fearless Responsibility

I T IS ESSENTIAL TO note that by "fearless leaders" we do not mean the leader who lacks self-awareness and is unwilling to acknowledge that serious threats to the organization and people within it are scary. Thus, fearless leadership is not about the irrational denial of reality. Rather it is about the leader who creates conditions of psychological safety in which everyone can identify and acknowledge mistakes, threats—and yes, fear—without succumbing to impulsive decision-making or paralysis. Fearless leaders, therefore, do not engage in the illusion that they alone can save the organization and the world; rather, they are willing to ask for help, acknowledge their mistakes, and, learning from every error, move on to encourage their colleagues with candor and decisiveness (Cancialosi, 2015).

Leaders in ordinary times are required to cope with change and challenges internal and external. In ordinary times, there are labor disputes, unhappy parents, and most importantly, students in need of care, encouragement, and support. And in ordinary times, educational leaders are preoccupied with safety for students and staff. But since the spring of 2020 and for many years into the future, educational systems have faced and will continue to face extraordinary challenges that demand fearless leadership. During times of prolonged stress, our bodies and minds can be burdened with unending fear, fatigue, and panic that leads to allostatic overload (Schwartz & Pines, 2020), a phenomenon that occurs when demand on our internal resources exceeds our capacity. The consequences affect even the most vital leader, with symptoms that include physical exhaustion, mental clumsiness and accompanying poor decision-making, and emotional fragility.

In this chapter we will explore the first and most incongruous challenge of the fearless leader who is called upon to make changes quickly and effectively—and that is deciding what will *not* change. Then we will consider the requirements for fearless presence, how leaders can convey authentic concern and vulnerability without transmitting the panic that stems from the perception of cluelessness in the leader. Closely linked to this is fearless communication, and the lessons of history and the 21st century on the necessity of sharing news, including bad news, in a candid and timely manner. Once the information has been gathered, or at least the best available if incomplete information, leaders must engage in fearless decision-making. This is far from perfect decision-making; it is a process that is at once decisive and simultaneously open to mid-course corrections and influence by new information and evolving understanding. Finally, we will consider fearless responsibility, the willingness of the leader to acknowledge mistakes and miscommunications clearly, immediately, and forthrightly.

THE CENTRAL MESSAGE: WHAT DOES NOT CHANGE

In a survey of the change leadership literature (D. Reeves, 2021), I found experts very willing to outline the three, five, seven, ten steps and more that are essential to change. Yet none of these scholars and leaders, so ready to talk about cultural change, digital change, and every other kind of change, addressed the first principle of fearless leadership, and that is addressing what will not change. Imagine that you are a new leader for a school or system that desperately needs change. Student achievement is low, buildings are in disrepair, and staff morale is low. Your immediate impulse may be to say, "There's a new sheriff in town, and there are going to be a lot of changes around here." However necessary those changes may be, it is worth considering that you probably had five predecessors in the previous four years who had the same mindset. They believed that everything was wrong and that everything in the system—people, policies, practices, and structures—needed to be fixed. After each short-lived tenure, they wondered, "What did I miss?" I would posit that what they probably missed were the glimmers of hope, the islands of excellence, that could have formed the foundation on which effective inside-out change could have been built. I have been in meetings with a new superintendent in which the very clear operating presumption of the new leadership team was that any person or practice associated with the previous regime was tainted, incompetent, and in need of replacement. This was the method employed by Robespierre and the Jacobins during the darkest days of the French Revolution, when the Committee of

Public Safety sent, depending on the data one wishes to believe, from 20,000 to 40,000 people to the guillotine—with accusation, arrest, sham trial, and execution happening within hours (McChrystal et al., 2018). Their leader, Maximillian Robespierre, soon followed with his own public humiliation and ritual death. One need not justify the excesses of the French nobility to oppose mass murder. Rather, the point is that too many leaders follow in the footsteps of Robespierre when they assume that their elevation to a leadership post empowers them to wipe out everything and everyone in their path without a thoughtful consideration of what does not need to change. It was possible to restore to the people the wealth accumulated by Louis XVI without killing him. We might do well to recall that in the years before the French Revolution, some of these ill-gotten riches were used to finance the American Revolution.

Let us return to the new school or system leader. Rather than the rhetoric about the new leaders and threats to the people and practices that preceded them, we might consider a different appeal:

> Colleagues, I want you to know that I've taken some time to learn about you. While I know that we all want to improve, we have a strong foundation on which to build. I have found some wonderful examples of values, teachers going the extra mile for students, strong parent connections, and exceptional commitments to integrity, teamwork, and service. I want you to know that I value these foundations and the people and practices that exemplify them. I'm going to be asking you to help to me identify and replicate our most effective practices that represent our values in action. I'm going to be asking you to

help me encourage and support people who might need a kind word or act of appreciation. Together, we will make progress.

These words do not minimize the need for change, but they render it a collaborative act rather than the act of the sole heroic leader who marches triumphantly into the conquered city equipped with a sword and a shield but is ill-equipped to make the changes that will bring hope and desperately needed improvements for students and the staff members who support them.

FEARLESS PRESENCE

In the leadership classic *Good to Great*, readers are reminded that the most successful leaders may not have the charisma that is stereotypically associated with great leadership; more often, they are self-effacing and modest (Collins, 2001). Modesty, however, does not imply tepid and doubt-filled presence. Rather, effective leaders must above all be authentic, neither exaggerating their prowess nor failing to step up to the challenges before them. Fearless presence is enhanced by four leadership actions (Baldoni, 2010).

First, keep score. This is particularly important in times of crisis. Without equivocation or temporizing, fearless leaders announce failures, deaths, illnesses, and injuries with the same candor that they announce recoveries and catastrophes avoided. From the days after the September 11, 2001 terrorist attacks through the financial crisis of 2007, to the COVID-19 pandemic of 2020, the most effective leaders provided credible data to their colleagues and the general public, making precisely clear the scope of the challenges and what needed to be done. Great educational leaders who have successfully led recoveries of schools, educational systems, and entire nations have done the same.

Second, the most effective leaders radiated command, leaving no doubt that they were responsible not only for recovery in the future but also for mistakes that inevitably occur. Young military officers in training learn that when there is any doubt about responsibility, they accept it without reservation. The phrase, "No excuse, sir" and "No excuse, ma'am" may sound anachronistic to 21st-century ears, but they are at the heart of the acceptance of responsibility that every person in command must embrace.

Third, leadership presence requires humility. These leaders share credit, admit what they don't know, and never commit the cardinal sin of claiming that they alone are the solution to enormous challenges.

Fourth, fearless leaders provide hope. This is not the fairytale hope of every problem being solved and every person living happily ever after. It is the hope in which leaders promise not only a brighter day in the future but also explain honestly the costs that will be borne by us all. In the Great Depression of the 1930s, Franklin Roosevelt famously announced in his inaugural speech that we had nothing to fear but fear itself. That line, historians tell us, received only mild applause. The greatest applause was reserved for Roosevelt's promises of action. He candidly addressed the present crisis with decisive action and set about creating a new future (Govindarajan & Faber, 2016). Though Roosevelt did not have the advantage of the insights from neuroscience of the 21st century, his leadership presence certainly suggested that he intuitively grasped these principles. The *Harvard Business Review* documented the impact of fear in the 1930s and the fears and uncertainties that grip the nation and world well into the 21st century. Humans are at least 25 times less intelligent, researchers found, when we are in the grip of our fears. We will reject anything that takes us out of comfort zones, retreating to reptilian instincts that served us better in fighting ancient predators than in working through the economic, medical, and political challenges of the 21st century (Goleman et al., 2013).

FEARLESS COMMUNICATION

It is difficult to communicate persuasively and calmly when one is running away from a predator. Research suggests five essentials for leadership communication. First, rather than deferring to governmental or other agencies that may sanitize or obscure information, leaders must be willing to give their colleagues and the public the information they need, when they need it. When leaders wait for perfect information, the vacuum of silence can be filled with our worst fears.

Second, communicate simply, clearly, and frequently. People in the midst of a crisis do not need a 32-point contingency plan. They need to know what individuals and teams must do now. Briefings should be daily or more frequently when necessary, excising jargon, excuse-making, and obscurity.

Third, our colleagues and the public need leaders with candor, not charisma. Every exaggeration, misstatement, and lie will be remembered and will invalidate future statements that might be true but were delivered by an untrustworthy source.

Fourth, leadership presence can supercharge resilience. This is accomplished not with rhetoric but with compelling recollections of how individuals, teams, and societies have bounced back from challenges in the past. We need inspiration not from fantasies but from reality, even those realities that may have been lost to memory. The great tragedy of a couple of generations that have been told that history is "just facts" is that they cannot easily draw on the wisdom of their ancestors. Leaders with a presence that taps into historical realities can transcend the generations to help us recall the greatness that is ours, not only on the battle-fields of generations past but also in Civil Rights marches, emergency rooms, and schools.

Fifth, leadership presence can help distill meaning from chaos. This is not the facile reassurance that "everything happens for a reason"; rather, it is our intrinsic search for meaning that defines the human spirit (Frankl, 1946).

FEARLESS DECISION-MAKING

In the previous chapter, we considered the elements of disciplined decision-making and the process leaders must engage in to identify advantages and disadvantages of every decision alternative. In President Kennedy's most important planet-saving decisions, he did not settle for the illusion of consensus and unanimity, but required debates to take place in front of him without filters or hierarchy. An analysis of crisis decisions by Harvard Business School researchers (Kerrissey & Edmondson, 2020) suggests that in reaction to crises ranging from the largest mass murder in the history of New Zealand to the COVID-19 pandemic, leaders ranging from Prime Minister Jacinda Ardern to local, state, and national leaders around the globe made decisions that elevated the long-term interests of their nations above the short-term demands of interest groups. Without fearless leadership, organizations can be paralyzed and unable to make the necessary decisions about strategy, people, and resource allocation. They essentially move from feckless to fearless (Merchant, 2012). These are the decisions that are made when there is a strong degree of trust between leaders and colleagues, and they create an environment in which bold moves can occur.

While careful comparison of the advantages and disadvantages is an essential attribute of fearless decision-making, it is essential to avoid the trap of analysis paralysis (Boss, 2015), a condition in which the fear of making wrong decisions causes leaders to avoid making essential decisions. Perfect information is never available, so leaders must balance the risks and rewards of every decision based on the best available evidence, not perfect evidence. Even when every shred of information available to the leader appears to be available, we remain flummoxed by the "unknown unknowns" discussed in the previous chapter.

Another block to fearless decision-making is the reluctance of leaders to engage in evaluation of alternatives. This is particularly true when leaders seek to generate decision alternatives through traditional brainstorming. Almost everyone has suffered through the brainstorming drill in which the rules require the generation of as many ideas as possible, including those that are evidently unworkable. The central rule of the process is "no judgment" so that as many ideas as possible are put forth. There is only one problem with traditional brainstorming: It doesn't work. The rules of brainstorming were articulated in an awful book, devoid of a shred of evidence, written by an advertising executive in the 1940s and published in many subsequent editions (Osborn, 1953). As early as 1960, academic studies revealed that this process was ineffective, yet brainstorming persisted as a method of generating solutions to vexing problems throughout the remainder of the 20th century and well into the 21st. A synthesis of the evidence against brainstorming (Reeves & Reeves, 2016) suggests an alternative in which ideas are generated not in a shouting session in which a facilitator frantically places ideas on the board, but with every participant writing down ideas in private. Then each idea is evaluated on the spot for relevance and applicability. This avoids the self-censorship that is the hallmark of traditional brainstorming. While it is a process that ruffles the sensibilities of those who find the judgment-free zone of traditional brainstorming a comfortable buffer from the world of debate, comparison, and evaluation—it is at the heart of fearless decision-making.

Making decisions in the face of imperfect information requires not only fearless leadership but also the willingness of the leader to assume responsibility when things go wrong. That sense of personal responsibility and the resistance against blaming others for decisions that are inevitably imperfect and outright failures is the subject to which we now turn our attention.

FEARLESS RESPONSIBILITY

Responsibility is often associated with results, but the achievement of goals is necessary but not sufficient for leadership success. In a global study of organizational performance that utilized interviews with thousands of leaders, Accenture found that success depends not only on delivery of results but also on continuous innovation, a commitment to sustainability, and trust. Organizations that succeeded in all three of these elements outperformed their peers by a factor of three. Performance is great, but without trust, innovation, and sustainability, the mere achievement of goals becomes a short-lived mirage (Shook, 2020).

Colleagues, neighbors, family, and friends will assess a leader's degree of responsibility using these criteria. First, they are motivated by acting in the interest of others, not opportunistically. Second, they build and maintain credibility by invariably acting in good faith, telling the truth, and fulfilling promises. Third, responsible leaders exhibit competence, capability, and capacity to meet the needs of the organization and the people within it. Fourth, people can rely on responsible leaders. They will make mistakes, but they can always be relied upon to be consistent and predictable based on their commitment to integrity and personal responsibility (Stevenson, 2020).

In this chapter we have explored the central message of fearless leadership—deciding what does *not* change. Even when facing the need for great changes, leaders must simultaneously identify and validate the practices and values that will endure and the people whose labor will be required to turn the page and get to the next level of success and recovery. Leadership does not require a regal presence. Rather, it requires the confidence and assurance that uncertainty and doubt are not our enemies but natural parts of the change process. Fearless communication requires not oratory but plainspoken truth. Fearless decision-making requires a dependence upon the lessons of the past, with leaders around the globe who have risen to unimaginable challenges in the 21st century and in times past. Fearless responsibility is not about recklessness without a hint of self-doubt but about the willingness to engage in imperfect decisions and then accept the blame and recrimination that inevitably result. In the next chapter we will consider the greatest challenge to leaders—change.

DISCUSSION QUESTIONS

1. Although some writers claim that "the only thing that is certain is change," think about what will *not* change in your school or organization. What are enduring values, principles, or practices that will be consistent no matter what the future holds?

2. When you think of "leadership presence," what comes to mind? Based on your experience with different leaders, what distinguishes the false from genuine leadership presence?

3. During challenging times, leaders must often communicate bad news. How do fearless leaders balance the need to instill confidence and trust while still delivering news that is distressing and may induce fear?

4. This chapter (and Chapter 7) considered how President John Kennedy dealt with two crises—the Bay of Pigs and the Cuban Missile Crisis—in two very different ways. Think of decisions that you or your leadership team have encountered that had good results and another decision with bad results. What can you learn about the decision-making process from those circumstances? How are they similar or dissimilar to the crises that President Kennedy faced and how he dealt with them?

5. Think about a decision that you or your leadership team has made for which the results are not clear. Whatever the results, explain who is ultimately responsible for that decision.

CHAPTER 10

FEARLESS CHANGE

In this chapter—

- How Fear Undermines Change
- The Myth of Buy-In
- The Value of Short-Term Wins
- Leading a Change-Ready Organization
- Ideas Before Personalities: When the Leader Changes

L EADERS ARE RESPONSIBLE FOR the success and progress of the organizations and people they lead, and as a result, leadership inevitably requires change. The alternative to change is not stability, but extinction (Llopis, 2014). Despite this self-evident proposition, people hate change. I have two good friends, one a school superintendent and the other a symphony orchestra conductor. Both are recognized as exceptionally talented in their fields and are internationally respected. Nevertheless, both have been fired, not just once, but on several occasions. Though the nature of the organizations differed, as did the geographical settings, the circumstances were identical. These leaders were hired to be change agents, and they succeeded in making changes that were precisely what the governing boards had requested. And then the governing board learned that change, even when wildly successful, was uncomfortable, unwelcome, and ultimately undesirable. It was as if the members of each organization said, "When we said we wanted change, we didn't expect that you would want *us* to change."

In this chapter we will explore the uncomfortable aspects of change, beginning with the truism that change requires entering unknown territory and working in an environment of uncertainty and unfamiliarity that can lead to fear—and that very fear undermines change. Change without fear is a fantasy, yet that fantasy is precisely what many governing-board members who engage a leader to be a change agent expect.

One of the truisms of change, at least in the eyes of people who don't have to lead change, is that in order to implement a change, the leader must gain buy-in from all stakeholder groups. This is a myth, though telling people that leaders do not need to, nor can they, gain buy-in from everyone is somewhat like telling a six-year-old that the tooth fairy doesn't exist. Although the child certainly is developing suspicion about this and other childhood myths, it nevertheless is painful to let these myths expire. Next, we will consider the value of short-term wins and contrast this with the futility of long-term strategic plans. If leaders are unwilling and unable to articulate what can be accomplished in 100 days, then it is doubtful that they can succeed over a longer time period.

It is not just the leader that must be ready for change. The organization itself must be sufficiently flexible and responsive to accept and implement change. This may involve changes in communication patterns, reporting relationships, and traditional hierarchies—all of which are heavily invested in the status quo. Change, even when clearly necessary, means a loss—a loss of previous practice, of dearly held patterns and behaviors, and often a loss of power because effective change may require power to be more widely shared throughout the organization. People do not give up power easily, especially when they have invested years or decades acquiring it. Finally, we will consider the relative importance of ideas and personalities. The real measure of the change-ready organization is the extent to which changes can continue after a transition in leadership. In personality-driven organizations, this transition spells doom for any meaningful change. In idea-driven organizations, change can endure through one leadership transition after another.

HOW FEAR UNDERMINES CHANGE

If ever there were a situation when fear would support change rather than undermine it, it would be the suggestions and requirements that people stay indoors, limit contact, and wear masks during a pandemic in which the failure to follow this advice could be fatal to oneself and loved ones. Nevertheless, Wharton Professor Jonah Berger suggests that people have anti-persuasion radar in which they're predisposed to reject even life-saving advice. Well before the COVID-19 pandemic, there was an abundance of advice about avoiding junk food, alcohol abuse, and addictive drugs—yet obesity and dependence upon drugs and alcohol continue to increase (Berger, 2020). We even have what Harvard researchers have called immunity to change (Keagan & Leahay, 2009), in which individuals and organizations expel changes just as the body attempts to expel toxins. One might think that avoiding death would be a sufficient rationale to get people to wear face masks during a pandemic, avoid junk food, and limit their consumption of alcohol and opioids. One hypothesis for why smart people do dumb things is that traditional intelligence tests do not measure our ability to behave rationally (Butler, 2017). And yet many people who excel in both intelligence and rational thinking do not behave intelligently and rationally. Think of physicians and attorneys who also smoke, drink excessively, drive recklessly, and are obese. It is neither a lack of information nor a cognitive deficit that leads to poor decision-making; rather, it is fear.

This countervailing fear that leads to irrational decision-making is the fear of losing control. At the very heart of resistance to change is fear, not of death or illness, but of the loss of agency. It is the reason that alcoholics and drug addicts risk their lives, relationships, careers, and futures. Each time they reach for a drink or a drug, they are elevating their need for personal control over conceding that control to others. This is why, in the spring of 2020, otherwise intelligent, caring, and decent people exposed themselves and family members to life-threatening illness by refusing to engage in the simple precautions of social distancing and wearing masks in public. It is easy to engage in stereotypes of people wearing Confederate flag emblems and waving "Live Free or Die" flags, apparently unaware of the provenance of that slogan. We would like to think that they are just uninformed sociopaths who don't care for themselves or their families. While such judgments are tempting, that does not explain the irrational behavior of intelligent, well-informed, kind, decent, and generous people, including perhaps a few readers of this book. I certainly know it applies to me. Despite some fairly significant accomplishments as a teacher, leader, and writer—I am plagued by memories of decisions that were ill-informed, destructive, and impulsive. It as if, in the old Sven and Ole joke, we continue to ride toward the train crossing while the locomotive is barreling down the track toward us, with the explanation that, "Sven told me just the other day that he had never seen a really good train wreck before."

Our imperviousness to change explains part of the reason for the supposed necessity that leaders gain buy-in—the apparent acceptance of change before they implement it is an illusion.

THE MYTH OF BUY-IN

There is a prevailing mythology of change leadership that if we just find the right blend of persuasion, research, and emotional appeal, the staff will embrace the changes leaders wish to make. This false belief is based on the myth of buy-in—that in order to implement effective change, leaders must first gain widespread agreement from the staff. When leaders tell me that they have buy-in from all of their staff members, one of two things is true. Either they are not really asking for significant change or, more likely, the real resistance is happening underground, out of the earshot of the leader. This is why the vast majority of change initiatives fail. One of the foremost global consultancy firms, McKinsey, has acknowledged that more than 70 percent of change efforts fail (Ewenstein, et al., 2015).

Change of any sort is difficult and painful. Change represents a loss—a loss of prior practices and a loss of an established comfort zone. Anyone who claims that they can make change easy or popular has never led a significant change effort. Pain-free organizational change falls into the same category as easy weight-loss and simple brain surgery. I am suggesting we toss aside the myth of buy-in and instead acknowledge the challenges and difficulties associated with change and address our colleagues in a respectful manner, even when they disagree with a proposed change.

I am not suggesting that leaders bully and intimidate subordinates into change. Rather, we must transform the conversation from a desperate appeal for agreement to a thoughtful, respectful, and reasoned approach to the uncertainty and difficulty that surround all change efforts. Consider, for example, the solid but unpopular research on nonfiction writing. When students write to describe, persuade, evaluate, and compare, it improves their performance in reading comprehension, mathematics, science, and social studies. Schools that have engaged in systematic writing—every subject, every grade, every month—have made substantial gains in student achievement (D. Reeves, 2020a). Despite the evidence, it's a hard sell. Teachers have full plates—too many standards, overburdened curricula, student behavior issues, and an unending stream of initiatives from helpful outsiders. "And now you want me to add writing? You've got to be kidding!"

Let's change the conversation. No more earnest appeals. No more inspirational speeches. No more imperious demands. Just a thoughtful and respectful dialogue that goes something like this: "We've all heard the research on the power of writing to improve student achievement, but I want you to know that I heard your skepticism very clearly. You are busy and besides, most of you are not trained as teachers of writing. So, I'm not asking you for buy-in right now. I'm just asking for a fair chance. You choose the day, you choose the writing prompt, and you choose how or whether to grade it. All I'm asking is that once each month for the next four months, you have a nonfiction writing prompt linked to your curriculum. Perhaps you will ask students to explain a graph in math, describe a map in social studies, compare two artists or pieces of music, or describe an experiment in science. I'm asking that you use our very brief, simplified rubric—it's only about one third of a page. We should all expect students to write coherently, spell correctly, and support their claim in every subject with evidence. You are the subject experts and can assess content however you wish. I promise that we'll then look at the results at the end of the semester and evaluate for ourselves whether the national research on writing is relevant to our school. To be clear, I know that many of you are skeptical, and I value and respect skeptics. Skeptics brought us the Age of Enlightenment. Skeptics brought us the scientific revolution. Skepticism is how we learn and grow. So, it's OK to be skeptical—but let's give this a fair try and learn together what works best for our students in our school."

I've seen similar progress in grading reform, a deeply emotional subject with strong opposition from many teachers. Rather than implement an overhaul in grading systems that inevitably creates tension among faculty and parents, start small. In the past few months, I've seen very skeptical teachers make presentations to their colleagues about small changes in their grading systems. "I wasn't ready to change everything," said one California high school science teacher. "But I just changed two things—I stopped using the average to calculate semester grades, and I went back to our old-fashioned A, B, C, D, F grading scale—just like we calculate grade-point averages, with A=4, B=3, C=2, D=1, and F=1. I got rid of the 100-point scale. That was it—just those two changes, and this semester, with the same curriculum and same assessments, I had more than 40 fewer Ds and Fs. It really made a difference. Students who used to fail were willing to show resilience, work hard, and achieve at higher levels. I also noticed that student behavior was significantly better because I didn't have students who had just emotionally checked out due to certain failure." I could have given a thousand speeches on grading that were not as effective as this one teacher speaking to his colleagues with evidence from students in his school. The success of small wins and incremental progress as the source of large-scale system change is the subject to which we now turn our attention.

THE VALUE OF SHORT-TERM WINS

In a comprehensive review of the elements of effective change (Clear, 2018), the author lays out a powerful evidence-based approach to how individuals and organizations change. It is not through massive changes, but through incremental improvements with measurable results. No Stalinist five-year plans. No bizarrely complicated strategic plans. No massive improvement plans that sit on the shelf, disconnected from the people responsible for implementing it. It's frequent actions, like asking students to engage in nonfiction writing just once a month—or small improvements in grading practices, like getting rid of the average—that are widely accepted as reasonable and that can show results in a single semester. While it is nearly impossible to gain meaningful buy-in in the threatening environment of huge changes, smaller changes accompanied by smaller wins can have a more positive impact on morale and achieve greater results in a shorter period of time. The impact of short-term wins on long-term results is most evident when we consider the virtues of 100-day plans (D. Reeves & Eaker, 2019). In this astonishingly short period of time, the Constitution of the United States was written, as was one of Dostoevsky's greatest novels. The origins of the turnaround from the Great Depression in the spring of 1933 were accomplished in fewer than 100 days. In brief, great accomplishments do not require Stalinist five-year plans but do require the focus and concentration that effective leadership can provide.

LEADING A CHANGE-READY ORGANIZATION

In *Deep Change Leadership: A Model for Renewing and Strengthening Schools and Districts* (D. Reeves, 2021), I suggest that leaders conduct a thorough assessment of their experiences with personal and organizational change. This analysis yields potential levels of change readiness. When leaders have a strong history of personal change—perhaps improvements in health, personal habits, or relationships—but the organization they serve does not share such a successful history, then they are in the quadrant labeled Ready for Learning. These leadership teams may need work on planning, communicating, and executing change. Moreover, the organization must create an evidence-based culture in which a clear and compelling case for change leads to a sense of urgency by every stakeholder. Finally, a commitment to clear and public data displays must be in place so that the results of the change can be shared widely, reinforcing the commitment and hard work of every person contributing to the change effort. Figure 10.1 illustrates four levels of change readiness.

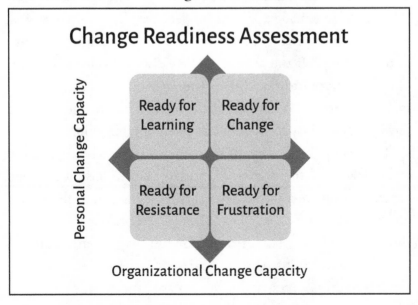

When neither the leaders nor the organization have much in the way of successful change experience, expect them to be ready for resistance. The most likely result of any new change initiative will be resistance, anger, undermining, or simply ignoring the effort. Without stakeholder support or leadership execution, these organizations will simply out-wait every new change initiative and the leaders who attempt to implement them.

There are cases when the organization is ready for change, but the leader is reluctant to change, either through personal fear of the repercussions of change or, more likely, a lack of personal experience in effective change. In these cases, there is a strong potential for frustration. Each time the organization gets ahead of the leader, and the ensuing change fails to be supported by senior leadership, change becomes less safe. Eventually, the organization will stop taking risks and migrate to the left-hand side of the matrix. The next leader will inherit an organization with severely compromised change readiness, and it will be time to rebuild trust and regain change capacity. An essential interview question for every leadership candidate is this: "Please tell me when you have made a significant personal change—where you were before the change, how you made the change, and how you are today." If the answer is, "I've always been perfect" or, "I've been trying to do a little better at work-life balance," this is not a person who has undergone significant change and will have the credibility to lead change in an organization.

The change-ready organization is one in which both the leadership team and the organization itself has demonstrated experience and prowess in effective change. When both the leader and the organization have exceptional change capacity, it is a model of resilience. This organization can adapt to environmental and cultural shifts, change strategies and form, innovate in services and resources, and create an atmosphere of excitement and engagement. It is not required that in this quadrant the organization has emerged from bankruptcy and the leader has given up smoking and alcohol, but it certainly is helpful that the organization has weathered reorganizations, implemented innovative ideas with both failures and successes, and has leaders with personal capacities for change.

IDEAS BEFORE PERSONALITIES: WHEN THE LEADER CHANGES

In idea-driven organizations, the essential changes are far more important than the identity of the individual leader. In the organizations I have led, I have always told my colleagues that if I were to be hit by a bus, I would hope that they would be sad but would hope even more that they remained employed. Ideas, I explained, are far more important than individual personalities. When leadership changes, either as a matter of planned transition or suddenly, it is imperative that the culture of the organization prizes ideas over personalities. We can view a departing leader with respect and affection, but it is the culture and ideas that remain that are most important (Lei, 2019).

In this chapter we have explored how fear undermines change and, in particular, how fear of losing control can exceed even fears of illness, injury, or death. Ivy-league educated Harley riders sometimes do not wear helmets. There may be many reasons to be upset with Harvard, Yale, and the graduates of the rest of the League, but their scrambled brains on the pavement is not one of them. Fear of the loss of control is a universal trait that respects no educational boundaries. The most common error made by leaders seeking changes is the pursuit of buy-in. They might as well burn incense and sacrifice to the gods of change than hope for buy-in, which is an illusion when it does appear, and even worse, contradicts how change really happens. Effective-change leaders know that behavior precedes belief, not the other way around. It is short-term wins—not institutional buy-in with a glacial pace of change—that transform and energize individuals and organizations. Changes in as short as 100 days can be and have been transformative for organizations and nations. In order to lead a change-ready organization, both the organization and the leadership team must have demonstrated competence in change. This includes not merely organizational changes, but the individual vulnerability of leaders to talk about how they personally overcame challenges and successfully led themselves before they sought to lead others. Finally, we considered the principle of ideas before personalities. Organizations must be able to survive leadership transitions, planned and unplanned. Principles, values, and ideas last; individual leaders never do.

In our final chapter we will consider the missing element in even very well-managed organizations, and that is systems thinking. We'll examine how decisions directed to one part of the system have unintended and unexpected impacts on other elements of the system.

DISCUSSION QUESTIONS

1. Think of a change—either personal or organizational—that you have observed in the past several years. Change implementation is almost never immediate. In your judgment, what delayed the final implementation of that change?
2. Leaders often have good intentions about gaining buy-in from staff members before making a change. Think of a change that needs to be made in your school or organization. What are the impediments to getting buy-in from staff members? What will the consequences be if you fail to get

buy-in? What will the consequences be if you fail to make the change?

3. Think of a change that you would like to make in your school or organization. What are some results that you could expect to see immediately—in fewer than 100 days?

4. The change-ready organization requires that both the organization and the individual leader be ready to change. Think of a change that you have successfully made, either personally or in your career. How did that successful change inform how your school or organization undertook a challenge that was underway?

5. Leadership turnover is inevitable in schools and organizations. What are the central ideas that propel necessary changes that will endure even after a transition in leadership?

CHAPTER 11.

PUTTING IT ALL TOGETHER: FEARLESS SYSTEMS

In this chapter—
- Defining Systems Thinking
- The Learning Organization Revisited
- Rapid Feedback Loops
- Certainty and Humility
- Envisioning the Future Without a Crystal Ball

PERHAPS YOU HAVE WANDERED into a county fair during the languorous days of summer, passing the prize-winning pies and jams, moving on to the 4-H lambs, hogs, turkeys, rabbits, and steers ready for auction and finally on to the midway past the deep-fried Oreos and nearly every other threat to cardiac health that a county fair can offer. Eventually, you found yourself on the lane filled with games, darts, rings, and shooting galleries. But the most frustrating game was Whac-A-Mole. The player has a mallet and earns points by hitting a mole as it pops up. But as quickly as one mole is subdued, another pops up elsewhere. The game ends, invariably, when the persistence of the moles outlasts the patience—and the wallet—of the player with the mallet. You can give the carnival barker more money, game after game, but you never beat the moles. The term "Whac-A-Mole" has entered the modern leadership lexicon to represent the impossible challenge of addressing different problems as they pop up. Playing Whac-A-Mole is the opposite of systems leadership. The game depends upon two common leadership conceits. First, that the leader is the only one with the mallet, and second, that the only way to solve the problem of the moles is to engage in an endless and futile series of mallet strikes. A systems thinker might, for example, unplug the game, denying the power source to the moles. A more serious example of looking beyond the immediately apparent rules of the game comes from the 1983 film *War Games* in which Joshua, the voice of the computer equipped to destroy the world, concludes "The only winning move is not to play" (Badham, 1983).

In this book, we have explored leadership systems that extend beyond the simplicity of cause and effect in which the leader makes a decision that leads to observable results. Sometimes that happens. Leaders close schools and the result is that students are not occupying the buildings. But more often, there are unanticipated results associated with a single decision. Anticipating these unexpected interactions is the result of systems thinking. Getting stuck in a single cause-result framework is an endless game of Whac-A-Mole.

At the center of fearlessness is the establishment and maintenance of trust. When trust is violated, not only does it affect an individual leader who made a decision without credible communication, but it also affects every decision by that leader and many other leaders associated with the untrustworthy communication. Resilience, too, is part of a system, with the ability of a school or system to bounce back from defeat. All these factors influence fearlessness in practice from the school to the system level.

After defining systems thinking, we will consider the requirements to inculcate this discipline through the creation of learning organizations. This requires not only an attentiveness to multiple causes for each effect and the influence of one part of the system on others but also on the development of real-time feedback loops throughout the system. We cannot, for example, only consider the impact of school closures on the facilities we call schools but also on homes and public spaces throughout the communities that schools serve. We cannot consider only the impact of school closures on the days and weeks during which those closures occur; we must also take into account the impact of the closings over months and years into the future and how learning, physical health, and emotional health of students and adults are affected. Recognizing that feedback can be confusing and contradictory, leaders must temper the certainty with which they make decisions with the humility that recognizes that we are always operating with imperfect and incomplete information. There are few checkmates available to leaders in which every allowable move of both players is completely transparent. We close with a consideration of how leaders create the most plausible future scenarios possible without the aid of a crystal ball.

DEFINING SYSTEMS THINKING

How can we tell if we are applying systems thinking in practice? Part of the answer lies in what we notice about our reactions to discussions. Leaders are often taught to follow the principle of parsimony. This is based on the rule of Occam's Razor, named after the 14th-century theologian who found the logical gymnastics of his contemporaries unnecessary and claimed that the simplest solution to a problem is likely the best. He died of the Black Plague in 1349 and might have pondered in his last days whether there might be more than a single cause for a single effect. The essence of systems thinking is a shift from "cause to effect" thinking to multiple causes and multiple effects (Kirsch et al., 2016). In fields as diverse as education, epidemiology, and astrophysics, this transformation in thinking is vital to advancing our understanding. Educational advertising is full of bivariate analysis in which vendors claim one cause—the program they are selling—for one effect, such as an increase in student test scores. But every teacher knows that students bring to their experience of any educational program a host of other factors, including nutrition, trauma, sleep deprivation, prenatal care, and previous education—all of which influence their results—and teachers reach this understanding without the benefit of a graduate course in multivariate statistics. Epidemiologists know that while a virus may cause a disease, patient vulnerability to that disease hinges on many other factors. Astrophysicists know that the gravitational pull of a star is only one of many influences on the movements of bodies surrounding it.

Here are some ways you can tell if you're engaging in systems thinking (Goodman, 2018):

- Are you asking different questions that extend beyond traditional causes? For example, if student absences are high, are you asking not only about calls from truant officers but also about the consistency and availability of transportation, about the presence of adults in the home in the hours before school to wake students up and prepare them for the school day, and about obligations in the nighttime hours after school for work, child care, and sibling care?

- Are you noticing simplistic answers to complex problems? If the answer is always, "We need more staff," or "We need more money," then however meritorious these requests might be, leaders will be stuck in a doom-loop of simplistic answers for complex problems if they do not engage in the systems-thinking discipline of multiple causality.
- Are you noticing mental models—the unstated assumptions—behind recommendations for solutions? The wisdom of toddlers who ask "why" a seemingly endless number of times is a valuable tool for the systems thinker.

While these questions are valuable for leaders, the system will not advance until the discipline of systems thinking extends throughout the organization. This is the path from the leader bearing the burden of systems thinking alone to the learning organization in which colleagues at every level engage in systems thinking.

THE LEARNING ORGANIZATION REVISITED

In the 1990s, MIT Senior Lecturer and founder of the Center for Organizational Learning Peter Senge cemented an international reputation as the foremost leadership thinker in systems thinking. He popularized the term "learning organization" with his seminal book *The Fifth Discipline*, updated and revised in subsequent editions (Senge, 2006). At a conference in Singapore where we had both keynoted before a global audience, Senge and I were standing in pouring rain waiting for a taxi back to our hotel. Not wanting to miss an opportunity to learn from such a distinguished expert, I suggested that we share a cab. During our brief ride, I asked Senge to give me the 20-minute version of learning organizations, because although I had studied his work for over a decade, I still found it sometimes confusing. Senge boiled it down to three big ideas. First, every part of a system influences every other part. Second, learning organizations notice these interactions and continually gain new knowledge. Third, and perhaps most importantly, making and admitting mistakes are keys for anyone who aspires to lead a learning organization. This gave me greater clarity than I had gained from hours of reading his work and listening to him speak.

Senge's vision of learning organizations has been the foundation for additional thoughtful work by leadership researchers. Three factors have limited the progress of systems thinking and the dominance of the learning organization (Garvin et al., 2008). While Senge's original work is almost three decades old, the foundations of systems thinking and the improvements by other scholars are profoundly important in the uncertain age of the 2020s. There are three important improvements to the original versions of systems thinking. First, people need clarity and specificity. When health and economic factors make forecasts impossible and subject to wildly varying assumptions, leaders and their colleagues need to identify "whatever" standards. That is, whether buildings are open, closed, or partially opened—whatever—here are the next steps we will take. Whether our employees continue, quit, or take medical leave—whatever—here are the staffing decisions we will make. While educational leaders, like leaders of every other organization from shops to theatrical troupes, are subject to the decisions of state and local authorities, we can nevertheless make some "whatever" decisions. This can be a great learning opportunity, as COVID-19 in 2020 and 2021 will not be the only time that uncertainty and unpredictability strike schools and other organizations. Second, the application of systems thinking and learning organizations must engage the entire organization. Just as *The Fifth Discipline* and its accompanying seminars and consulting engagements were largely aimed at CEOs, the lessons of distributed leadership articulated by Harvard Professor Richard Elmore demonstrate that any leadership system requires wide adoption not merely by superintendents with titular authority, but throughout the system, including by building administrators and teacher-leaders. (Gehram, 2008). The third flaw in the implementation of the first wave of systems thinking and learning organizations was the lack of reliable assessment systems. Organizations throughout the public and private spheres are littered with compelling concepts that were never implemented successfully for lack of a clear standard of accountability for translating leadership knowledge into actions at every level.

RAPID FEEDBACK LOOPS

Here's an experiment perhaps better executed in your mind than in practice. At the next anniversary with a spouse or loved one, prepare a sumptuous dinner accompanied by lovely flowers and perhaps some favorite music. About halfway through this celebratory meal, take out a piece of paper and say, "Sweetheart, it's time for your annual performance review." Do let me know where those flowers wind up when the conversation is concluded.

In this context, infrequent feedback is absurd and even harmful. But it is precisely this pattern of feedback that afflicts organizations and especially schools all the time. We provide annual and perhaps monthly feedback to students and teachers with little more advancement in thinking than the builders of Stonehenge 5,000 years ago. Let's consider a practical example in schools: attendance. We know that this is an *a priori* variable—that is, we can't measure learning if students are not there. We cannot hold teachers accountable for their impact on students who are absent. We cannot evaluate curriculum for students who do not use it. Attendance happens before everything else, so it's worth studying. In too many systems, attendance, like the unfortunate romantic dinner described above, is an annual mark in the accountability report. This is somewhat like an autopsy, during which wise people can observe some very interesting information, but the procedure rarely does much good for the patient. In some especially thoughtful districts, attendance is studied monthly so that schools that are making progress can share their most effective attendance practices with others. But in the very best schools, principals have the "60-second report," in which, a single minute after the bell has rung, the principal has the name and phone number of every absent student. In a stand-up meeting, the principal and every staff member not in front of students is calling all the students on the list. I've watched these meetings in a high-poverty urban school with nearly 1,000 students, and every absent student was called within 20 minutes. Some students missed the bus; others were asleep; others had parents who either overslept or who were not at home. But in every case, the principal knew not only that the students were absent but also why they were absent and what the school could do about it. Notice the contrast between this approach and the lazy robot-calls in the afternoon or calls by secretaries or attendance officers long after the school day has started. The 60-second report conveys a sense of urgency to students, families, and the entire staff that *nothing else in school happens* unless students are present.

Similarly, rapid feedback loops can be provided to teachers. There is no evidence that teachers are "evaluated into better performance," despite the millions of dollars devoted to laborious and inaccurate evaluation systems. Most of these systems are contrived, with only a couple of hours observed out of 180 classroom days, and the dates and times of these observations are announced, preventing any sort of authentic classroom experience for the teacher, students, or observer. A far better approach is the frequent mini-observation (K. Marshall, 2019) in which observers gain a much clearer picture of real classroom environments and teachers receive much more accurate and immediate feedback on their performance. Using very simple rubrics (available as free downloads at MarshallMemo.com), instructional coaches, administrators, and other observers can provide feedback to teachers with clear instructions for improvement without the need for lengthy written reports.

The manner in which we provide feedback to leaders is often worse than worthless where, the higher the rank and the longer the tenure of the leader, the greater the ambiguity of the evaluations and the longer the intervals between performance and assessment (D. B. Reeves, 2021). A better way to provide feedback to leaders, including support before prospective leaders even take on the responsibilities of leadership, is the rubric-based Leadership Performance Matrix (available as a free download at CreativeLeadership.net).

CERTAINTY AND HUMILITY

However precise or imprecise, fast or slow, the feedback a leader receives, it will certainly be imperfect. Therefore, while a leader must make decisions with the greatest degree of confidence possible, it is also necessary to approach each decision with the perspective of humility. If a decision needs revision or requires a complete change, it will be easier to do so if the organization has the discipline of systems thinking. Every move at every level of the organization from every member—whether directly involved in a decision or not—will be scrutinized when the decision is wrong. But with systems thinking, the environment changes from one of shifting blame to one of shared learning.

This means that leaders do not gloat about their successes, nor are they looking for scapegoats when there are failures. They succeed and learn as a team.

ENVISIONING THE FUTURE WITHOUT A CRYSTAL BALL

Leaders who failed to predict the impact of the COVID-19 pandemic and the subsequent economic fallout had lots of company, as confident predictions have a long history of being preposterously wrong (Dreher, 2020):

- 1876: The telephone has no inherent value.
- 1895: Sensible and reliable women do not need to vote.
- 1946: The television has no long-term future because people will grow tired of staring at a box for hours.
- 1954: Cigarettes, according to the Negational Cancer Institute, have only a minimal impact on lung cancer.
- 1962: The Beatles are not worth listening to and guitar music is on the way out.
- 1969: Great Britain isn't ready for a woman Prime Minister, said Margaret Thatcher, who was selected for that post ten years later.
- 1984: Michael Jorden isn't worth drafting because he isn't seven feet tall.
- 1996: Children aren't interested in witches and wizards—the excuse for rejecting the Harry Potter series.

These are easy to ridicule, just as are the leaders who were insufficiently prescient to see the future about any unexpected event. But as a world poker champion (Duke, 2019) reminds us, one can have a successful outcome based on terrible strategy, and one can lose a pot of money with a good strategy. Decision-making is, she concludes, a combination of strategy and chance.

And people who evaluate leadership decisions solely based on outcomes are perilously likely to overestimate the skill of the decision-maker and underestimate the role of chance. The executives who rejected Harry Potter and the Beatles were playing the odds, and although in retrospect their decisions were spectacularly wrong, most leaders must focus on hundreds, perhaps thousands, of decisions and cannot afford the luxury of either basking in the glow of the decisions with great outcomes or wallowing in the mire of the bad outcomes. They must play the hand that they are dealt.

Without a crystal ball, and without cheating with marked cards, what are leaders to do? Well before the COVID-19 outbreak and economic collapse of 2020, for example, many economists forecast that the long-running economic surge and bull market that accompanied it would not last forever (Kelleher, 2018). Despite their record of consistent growth, for example, we know that trees do not grow to the sky. The same is true of markets, children, and toenails. The absence of perfect prediction does not invalidate the practice of creating models; rather, it is a clarion call for us to be modest and judicious in the creation of models. Fearless systems are not reckless; rather, they are carefully constructed, considering both input from the past and a continuing stream of feedback that may or may not support the leader's original decisions and assumptions.

What does this mean for schools? It is not possible to be a teacher or educational leader without being an optimist. Like the birth of a child, every new school year brings with it both hope and apprehension, with emotions ranging from "She will be president someday!" to "How in the world are we going to get through this?" I will tell you precisely how we get through this. We have placed a bet on the future—the future of that child, of our families, and of the world. As Annie Duke reminds us, not every hand is a winner, but we play the long game when we bet on children and students. Only those least aware of the world around them assume an unbroken string of successes uninterrupted by disappointment and failure. But we could not remain in the world of education if we did not know deep in our bones that after tears are dried, skinned knees are soothed, and hurt feelings are mended, we see a better future. From the Black Plague in the 14th century to the Spanish Flu in the 20th century, from the Great Depression in the 20th century to the Great Recession in the 21st century—predictions of the demise of society have been of, well, epidemic proportions. But those predictions all had one thing in common: They were wrong, and the breathless rhetoric behind the predictions was not leavened by an understanding of the resilience of people, societies, and most especially, children.

DISCUSSION QUESTIONS

1. What is the highest-leverage factor in your school or organization—that is, the factor that if you change that one thing, it will influence every other part of the organization, and if you fail to change that one thing, efforts at change in other parts of the system will fail?

2. Learning organizations require the recognition that some things are not working—that is, identifying and learning from mistakes. What is a mistake that now affects your school or organization that must be recognized to establish a learning organization?

3. Systems leadership requires rapid feedback. What are some important areas where you now receive feedback at the end

of the year (or later) that could be accelerated so that leaders and teachers have the information in time to react to it and improve performance?

4. Think of some descriptions of your school or organization that have been made with certainty either by you or others, some of which turned out not to be true. What led to the certainty? What ultimately led you to challenge that certainty?

5. It's easy to take pot shots at the failed predictions of the past. Given that predictions require modesty and circumspection, what predictions can you make about the future of your school or organization?

ABOUT THE AUTHOR

Douglas Reeves is the author of more than 40 books including, most recently, *Achieving Equity and Excellence: Immediate Results from the Lessons of High-Poverty, High-Success Schools* (2020) and *Deep Change Leadership: A Model for Renewing and Strengthening Schools and Districts* (2021), both of which were published by Solution Tree Press. He has written more than 100 articles on education and leadership appearing in *Educational Leadership, School Administrator, Principal Leadership, The Learning Professional, American School Board Journal*, and many other publications. Twice named to the Harvard University Distinguished Authors Series, Doug received the Contribution to the Field Award from the National Staff Development Council (now Learning Forward) and was named the Brock International Laureate for his contributions to education. He is the founder of the nonprofit Equity and Excellence Institute in Boston, serving schools and educational institutions throughout the world.

Doug tweets @ DouglasReeves and blogs at CreativeLeadership. net

REFERENCES

Allen, S. (2018, February 15). *It's time to rethink how you brainstorm, according to this famous leadership expert.* Swirled. https://swirled.com/adam-grant-brainstorming-advice/

Alliance for Excellent Education. (2015). *The graduation effect.* Alliance for Excellent Education. http://impact.all4ed.org

Amabile, T., & Kramer, S. (2011). The power of small wins. *Harvard Business Review*, May 2011, 70–81.

Anderson, K. (2019, April 29). *How access to technology can create equity in schools.* Digital Promise. https://digitalpromise.org/2019/04/29/equity-in-schools-access-technology/

Badham, J. (Director). (1983). *War Games* [Motion picture]. United Artists.

Baldoni, J. (2010, May 5). Use your leadership presence to inspire. *Harvard Business Review,* May 2010. https://hbr.org/2010/05/use-your-leadership-presence-t

Barron, R. (n.d.). *Barriers to effective communication: Implications for the cockpit.* Airline Safety. http://www.airlinesafety.com/editorials/BarriersToCommunication.htm

Berger, J. (2020, April 20). How to persuade people to change their behavior. *Harvard Business Review.* https://hbr.org/2020/04/how-to-persuade-people-to-change-their-behavior

Blinder, A. (2015, April 1). Atlanta educators convicted in school cheating scandal. *The New York Times.* https://www.nytimes.

com/2015/04/02/us/verdict-reached-in-atlanta-school-test-ing-trial.html

Blumenthal, J. A., Smith, P. J., & Hoffman, B. M. (2012). Is exercise a viable treatment for depression? *ACSMs Health and Fitness Journal, 16*(4), 14–21. https://doi.org/10.1249/01. FIT.0000416000.09526.eb

Boss, J. (2015, March 20). How to overcome the "analysis paralysis" of decision-making. *Forbes.* https://www.forbes.com/sites/jeffboss/2015/03/20/how-to-overcome-the-analysis-paralysis-of-decision-making/#39cb0b321be5

Bouchard, T. (2019, January 27). *The value of our mistakes.* Psych Central. https://psychcentral.com/blog/the-value-of-our-mistakes/

Bowman, T. (2017, September 1). *3 Steps to combat anxiety and build your resilience to stress.* Goalcast. https://www.goalcast.com/2017/09/01/3-steps-to-combat-anxiety-build-resilience-stress/

Brow, A. (2014). *The myth of the strong leader: Political leadership in the modern age.* Basic Books.

Busteed, B. (2019, April 30). This will be the biggest disruption in higher education. *Forbes.* https://www.forbes.com/sites/brandonbusteed/2019/04/30/this-will-be-the-biggest-disruption-in-higher-education/#1d558ea2608a

Butler, H. (2017, October 3). Why do smart people do foolish things? *Scientific American.* https://www.scientificamerican.com/article/why-do-smart-people-do-foolish-things/

Camera, L. (2020, April 1). Disconnected and disadvantaged: Schools race to give students access. *U.S. News & World Report.* https://www.usnews.com/news/education-news/articles/2020-04-01/schools-rush-to-get-students-internet-access-during-coronavirus-pandemic

Cancialosi, C. (2015, November 1). The myth of fearless leadership: How to lead when you're afraid. *Forbes*. https://www.forbes.com/sites/chriscancialosi/2015/11/01/the-myth-of-fearless-leadership-how-to-lead-when-youre-afraid/#-7b1ec27b4f25

Chase, C. (2014, October 25). *Creative by nature*. Creative Systems Thinking. https://creativesystemsthinking.wordpress.com/2014/10/25/every-child-is-an-artist-by-nature/

Cherry, K. (2019, December 7). *Locus of control and your life*. Very Well Mind. https://www.verywellmind.com/what-is-locus-of-control-2795434

Clancy, C. (2020). *Treating depression with cognitive behavioral therapy*. JourneyPure. https://journeypureriver.com/treating-depression-cognitive-behavioral-therapy/

Clark, J. (2020, March 26). *Structure, self-care important for parents and kids during the Coronavirus pandemic*. WFPL News Louisville. https://wfpl.org/structure-self-care-important-for-parents-and-kids-during-the-coronavirus-pandemic/

Clear, J. (2018). *Atomic habits: An easy and proven way to build good habits and break bad ones*. Penguin Publishing Group.

Collins, J. C. (2001). *Good to great: Why some companies make the leap. . . and others don't*. HarperCollins.

Conversano, C., Rotondo, A., Lensi, E., Della Vista, O., Arpone, F., & Reda, M. A. (2010). Optimism and its impact on mental and physical well-being. *Clinical Practice & Epidemiology in Mental Health, 2010*(6), 25–29. https://doi.org/10.2174/1745017901006010025

Covey, S. M. R., & Conant, D. R. (2016, July 18). The connection between employee trust and financial performance. *Harvard Business Review*. https://hbr.org/2016/07/the-connection-between-employee-trust-and-financial-performance

Denyer, D. (2017). *Organizational resilience: A summary of academic evidence, business insights and new thinking.* BSI and Cranfield University. https://www.bsigroup.com/LocalFiles/EN-HK/Organisation-Resilience/Organizational-Resilience-Cranfield-Research-Report.pdf

Dipto, A. (n.d.). *What is modulus of resilience? Calculation and unit.* Civil Engineering. https://civiltoday.com/structural-engineering/260-what-is-modulus-of-resilience-calculation-unit

Dostoevsky, F. (1866). *Crime and punishment.* Barnes & Noble.

Dreher, B. (2020). 12 Historical predictions that completely, utterly missed the mark. *Reader's Digest.* https://www.readersdigest.ca/culture/worst-predictions/

DuFour, R., DuFour, R., Eaker, R., & Many, T. (2006). *Learning by doing: A handbook for professional learning communities at work.* Solution Tree.

DuFour, R., & Reeves, D. (2016). The Futility of PLC Lite. *Phi Delta Kappan, 97*(6), 69–71.

Duke, A. (2019). *Thinking in bets: Making smarter decisions when you don't have all the facts.* Penguin Publishing Group.

Eberstadt, J. (2020). *Biased: Uncovering the hidden prejudice that shapes what we see, think, and do.* Penguin Publishing Group.

Edmondson, A. C. (2018). *The fearless organization: Creating psychological safety in the workplace for learning, innovation, and growth.* Wiley.

Engleman, J. B., Meyer, F., Ruff, C. C., & Fehr, E. (2019). The neural circuitry of affect-induced distortions of trust. *Science Advances, 5*(3). https://doi.org/10.1126/sciadv.aau3413

Ericsson, A., & Pool, R. (2016). *Peak: Secrets from the new science of expertise.* Houghton Mifflin Harcourt.

Eva, A. L. (2017, November 28). Why we should embrace mistakes in school. *The Greater Good Magazine.*

https://greatergood.berkeley.edu/article/item/
why_we_should_embrace_mistakes_in_school

Ewenstein, B., Smith, W., & Sologar, A. (2015, July 1). *Changing change management*. McKinsey and Company. https://www.mckinsey.com/featured-insights/leadership/ changing-change-management#

Faueh, S. (2020, April 27). *NAS Annual Meeting: Experts discuss COVID-19 pandemic and science's response*. The National Academies of Science, Engineering, and Medicine. https:// www.nationalacademies.org/news/2020/04/nas-annual-meeting-experts-discuss-covid-19-pandemic-and-sciences-response

Feeding America. (2020). *What happens when a child faces hunger?* Feeding America. https://www.feedingamerica.org/ hunger-in-america/child-hunger-facts

Feintzeig, R. (2014, October 31). Flexibility at work: Worth skipping a raise? *Wall Street Journal*. https://blogs.wsj.com/atwork/2014/10/31/ flexibility-at-work-worth-skipping-a-raise/

Fessler, L. (2018, April 30). *The best leaders aren't optimists*. Quartz at Work. https://qz.com/work/1263261/ the-best-leaders-and-bosses-arent-optimists/

Frankl, V. (1946). *Man's search for meaning*. Beacon Press.

Frei, F., & Moriss, A. (2020). Begin with trust: The first step to becoming a genuinely empowering leader. *Harvard Business Review, 98*(3), 112–121.

Fuller-Thompson, E., Agbeyaka, S., LaFond, M. L., & Bern-Klug, M. (2016). Flourishing after depression: Factors associated with achieving complete mental health among those with a history of depression. *Psychiatry Research, 242*, 111–120. https://doi.org/org/10.1016/j.psychres.2016.04.041

Gallo, C. (2020, April 17). Finding the right words in a crisis. *Harvard Business Review*. https://hbr.org/2020/04/finding-the-right-words-in-a-crisis

Garvin, D. A., Edmondson, A. C., & Gino, F. (2008, March). Is yours a learning organization? *Harvard Business Review*. https://hbr.org/2008/03/is-yours-a-learning-organization

Gehram, E. (2008, May 29). *Building a new structure for school leadership*. Usable Knowledge. https://www.gse.harvard.edu/news/uk/08/05/building-new-structure-school-leadership

Gellman, I. F. (2015, December 5). *It's time to stop saying that JFK inherited the Bay of Pigs operation from Ike*. History News Network. https://historynewsnetwork.org/article/161188

Gewertz, C. (2020, April 20). Exhausted and grieving: Teaching during the Coronavirus crisis. *Miami Times*. https://www.miamitimesonline.com/covid-19_hub/exhausted-and-grieving-teaching-during-the-coronavirus-crisis/article_d494c94c-8357-11ea-bcb7-075cf66f7c06.html

Glaser, B. (2015, April). The irrationality of Alcoholics Anonymous. *The Atlantic*. https://www.theatlantic.com/magazine/archive/2015/04/the-irrationality-of-alcoholics-anonymous/386255/

Global Initiative to End All Corporal Punishment of Children. (2016, June). *Corporal punishment of children: Review of research on its impact and associations*. http://endcorporalpunishment.org/wp-content/uploads/research/Research-effects-review-2016-06.pdf

Godin, S. (2012). *The Icarus deception: How high will you fly?* Penguin Publishing Group.

Goleman, D., Boyatzis, R., & McKee, A. (2013). *Primal leadership, with a new preface by the authors: Unleashing the power of emotional intelligence*. Harvard Business Review Press.

Goodman, M. (2018). *Systems thinking: What, why, when, where, and how?* The Systems Thinker. https://thesystemsthinker. com/systems-thinking-what-why-when-where-and-how/

Gopnik, A. (2016, May). Little scientists: Babies have scientific minds. *Scientific American.* https://www.scientificamerican. com/article/little-scientists-babies-have-scientific-minds/

Govindarajan, V., & Faber, H. (2016, May 4). What FDR knew about managing fear in times of change. *Harvard Business Review.* https://hbr.org/2016/05/ what-fdr-knew-about-managing-fear-in-times-of-change

Grant, A. (2013). *Give and take: A revolutionary approach to success.* Viking.

Green, E. L. (2020, May 15). DeVos funnels coronavirus relief funds to favored private and religious schools. *The New York Times.* https://www.nytimes.com/2020/05/15/ us/politics/betsy-devos-coronavirus-religious-schools. html?searchResultPosition=1

Grieve, V. M. (2018). *Little Cold Warriors: American childhood in the 1950s.* Oxford University Press.

Guskey, T. (2014). *On your mark: Challenging the conventions of grading and reporting.* Solution Tree Press.

Hansen, M. T., Amabile, T. M., Snook, S. A., & Craig, N. (2018). *Purpose, meaning, and passion.* Harvard Business Review Press.

Harvard Health Letter. (2019, March 25). *Exercise is an all-natural treatment to fight depression: Exercise is as effective as drugs in some cases.* https://www.health.harvard.edu/mind-and-mood/ exercise-is-an-all-natural-treatment-to-fight-depression

Harvard Women's Health Watch. (2012, February). *Healing yourself after injury, illness, or surgery.* https:// www.health.harvard.edu/mind-and-mood/ healing-yourself-after-injury-illness-or-surgery

Henley, W. E. (1888). *Invictus.* https://www.poetryfoundation. org/poems/51642/invictus

Huang, L. (2020). *Edge: Turning adversity into advantage.* Penguin Publishing Group.

Hurleuy, K. (2020). *Stress vs. anxiety: How to tell the difference.* Psycom. https://www.psycom.net/stress-vs-anxiety-difference

Israel, M. (2015). *From chaos to coherence: Managing stress while teaching.* Education World. https://www.educationworld. com/a_admin/admin/admin413.shtml

Itzchakov, G., & Krueger, A. (2018, March 17). The power of listening in helping people change. *Harvard Business Review.* https://hbr.org/2018/05/ the-power-of-listening-in-helping-people-change

Johnson, L. (2020). *Resilience: The art of bouncing back.* Cognitive Behavior Therapy Center. https://cognitivebehaviortherapy-center.com/resilience/

Judeh, M. (2016). The influence of organizational trust on job performance: Mediating role of employee engagement. *International Journal of Business Research, 16*(5), 53–66. https:// doi.org/10.18374/IJBR-16-5.4

Junger, S. (2016). *Tribes: On homecoming and belonging.* HarperCollins Publishers.

Kafka, F. (1925). *The trial.* Penguin Random House.

Kang, H.-J., Kee, K.-Y., & Kim, S.-W. (2014). Impact of anxiety and depression on physical health condition and disability in an elderly Korean population. *Psychiatry Investigation, 14*(3), 240–248. https://doi.org/10.4306/pi.2017.14.3.240

Karson, M. (2014, January 14). Punishment doesn't work. *Psychology Today.* https://www.psychologytoday.com/us/ blog/feeling-our-way/201401/punishment-doesnt-work

Keagan, R., & Leahay, L. L. (2009). *Immunity to change: How to overcome it and unlock the potential in yourself and your organization.* Harvard Business Review Press.

Kelleher, K. (2018, November 21). U.S. economy will slow in 2019, may enter recession in 2020, economists forecast. Trump administration disagrees. *Fortune.* https://fortune.com/2018/11/21/us-economy-slow-2019-recession-2020-economist-forecast/

Kelly, W. (2018, April 25). Why punishment doesn't reduce crime. *Psychology Today.* https://www.psychologytoday.com/us/blog/crime-and-punishment/201804/why-punishment-doesnt-reduce-crime

Kennedy, R. (2020, April 24). *Corporal punishment: 2019 update.* Private School Review. https://www.privateschoolreview.com/blog/corporal-punishment-2019-update

Kent, S. (2020, March 20). *How COVID-19 could fuel school choice.* redefinED. https://www.redefinedonline.org/2020/03/how-covid-19-could-fuel-school-choice/

Kerrissey, M. J., & Edmondson, A. C. (2020, April 13). What good leadership looks like during this pandemic. *Harvard Business Review.* https://hbr.org/2020/04/what-good-leadership-looks-like-during-this-pandemic

Kirsch, V., Bildner, J., & Walker, J. (2016, July 25). Why social ventures need systems thinking. *Harvard Business Review.* https://hbr.org/2016/07/why-social-ventures-need-systems-thinking

Kouzes, J. M., & Posner, B. Z. (2011). *Credibility: How leaders gain and lose it; why people demand it.* Jossey-Bass.

Kuzma, C., & Jackson Cheadle, C. (2019, November 26). How to set new goals when you're injured to come back stronger. *Runners' World.* https://www.runnersworld.com/health-injuries/a29961641/rebound-train-your-mind-to-bounce-back-stronger-from-sports-injuries/

Lafley, A. G., Martin, R., Rivkin, J., & Siggelkow, N.

(2012, September). Bringing science to the art of strategy. *Harvard Business Review.* https://hbr.org/2012/09/bringing-science-to-the-art-of-strategy

Larson, E. (2020). *The splendid and the vile: A saga of Churchill, family, and defiance during the blitz.* Crown Publishing.

Lei, L. (2019, January 14). Make sure morale doesn't suffer when a favorite team member leaves. *Harvard Business Review.* https://hbr.org/2019/01/make-sure-morale-doesnt-suffer-when-a-favorite-team-member-leaves

Literary Devices. (n.d.). *Curiosity killed the cat.* https://literarydevices.net/curiosity-killed-the-cat/

Llopis, G. (2014, March 24). Every leader must be a change agent or face extinction. *Forbes.* https://www.forbes.com/sites/glennllopis/2014/03/24/every-leader-must-be-a-change-agent-or-face-extinction/#1251ec2c4e0f

MacDevey, M. (2018, April 26). *System redesign Part I: Why it matters.* The Tower Foundation. https://thetowerfoundation.org/2018/04/26/system-redesign-part-i-why-it-matters-html/

MacKay, J. (2019, January 17). The myth of multitasking: The ultimate guide to getting more done by doing less. *RescueTime.* https://blog.rescuetime.com/multitasking/

Mallik, A., Mallik, L., & Keerthi, D. S. (2019). Impact of Employee Morale on Organizational Success. *International Journal of Recent Technology and Engineering (IJRTE), 8*(4), 3289–3293. https://doi.org/10.35940/ijrte.D8070.118419

Mankins, M., & Garton, E. (2017). *Time, talent, energy: Overcome organizational drag and unleash your team's productive power.* Harvard Business Review Press.

Marchione, M. (2020, April 21). More deaths, no benefit from malaria drug in VA virus study. *AP News.* https://apnews.com/a5077c7227b8eb8b0dc23423c0bbe2b2

Marlow, A. (2017, March). *7 Strategies for dealing with a depressive episode.* Healthline. https://www.healthline.com/health/depression/strategies-for-dealing-with-depressive-episode#1

Marshall, K. (2019, February 20). *Rethinking the way we coach, evaluate, and appreciate teachers.* Thomas B. Fordham Institute. https://fordhaminstitute.org/national/commentary/rethinking-way-we-coach-evaluate-and-appreciate-teachers

Marshall, M.-L. (2018, October). *The symbiotic relationship between trust and innovation.* Fujitsu. https://www.i-cio.com/big-thinkers/rachel-botsman/item/the-symbiotic-relationship-between-trust-and-innovation

Mayo Clinic. (2019, April 4). *Stress management.* https://www.mayoclinic.org/healthy-lifestyle/stress-management/in-depth/stress-symptoms/art-20050987

McChrystal, S., Eggers, J., & Mangone, J. (2018). *Leaders: Myth and reality.* Penguin Publishing Group.

McGuffey, W. H. (1879). *McGuffey's third eclectic reader, revised edition.* Wiley

Merchant, N. (2012, February 8). Yahoo's shakeup demands fearlessness. *Harvard Business Review.* https://hbr.org/2012/02/yahoos-shakeup-demands-fearles

Merriam-Webster Dictionary. (n.d.). *Hobson's choice.* https://www.merriam-webster.com/dictionary/Hobson%27s%20choice

Modono, J. (2017). The trust factor. *Educational Leadership,* 74(8). http://www.ascd.org/publications/educational-leadership/may17/vol74/num08/The-Trust-Factor.aspx

Mullane, P. (2017, August 15). *What the Cuban Missile Crisis can teach us about decision-making.* Harvard Business School Online. https://online.hbs.edu/blog/post/what-the-cuban-missile-crisis-can-teach-us-about-decision-making

National Institute on Drug Abuse. (2010, September).

Comorbidity: Addiction and other mental illnesses. https://d14rmgtrwzf5a.cloudfront.net/sites/default/files/rrcomorbidity.pdf

Neeley, T. (2018, January 29). How to build trust with colleagues you rarely see. *Harvard Business Review.* https://hbr.org/2018/01/how-to-build-trust-with-colleagues-you-rarely-see

Oaklander, M. (2015, May 21). The science of bouncing back. *Time Magazine.* https://time.com/3892044/the-science-of-bouncing-back/

Osborn, A. F. (1953). *Applied imagination: Principles and procedures of creative thinking.* Scribner's Sons.

Ouslis, N. (2019, February 11). Trust in leadership—one key factor during organizational change. *Science for Work.* https://scienceforwork.com/blog/trust-in-leadership-change/

Phillips, O. (2015, March 30). Revolving door of teachers costs schools billions every year. *NPR.* https://www.npr.org/sections/ed/2015/03/30/395322012/the-hidden-costs-of-teacher-turnover

Ravitch, D. (2010). *The death and life of the great American school system: How testing and choice are undermining education.* Basic Books.

Reeves, D. (2018). Seven keys to restoring the teacher pipeline. *Educational Leadership,* 75(8). http://www.ascd.org/publications/educational-leadership/may18/vol75/num08/Seven-Keys-to-Restoring-the-Teacher-Pipeline.aspx

Reeves, D. (2020a). *Achieving equity and excellence: Immediate results from the lessons of high-poverty, high-success schools.* Solution Tree Press.

Reeves, D. (2020b). Supercharged cabinet meetings: Establishing norms, recording commitments, and requiring evidence for the body of senior leaders who advise the superintendent. *School Administrator* 4(77), 24–27.

Reeves, D. (2021). *The new model of change leadership.* Solution Tree Press.

Reeves, D. B. (2010). *Transforming professional development into student results.* Association for Supervision & Curriculum Development.

Reeves, D. B. (2016). *Elements of grading: A guide to effective practice* (2nd ed). Solution Tree Press.

Reeves, D. B. (2021). *The learning leader* (2nd ed). Association for Supervision & Curriculum Development.

Reeves, D., & Eaker, R. (2019). *100-day leaders: Turning short-term wins into long-term success in schools.* Solution Tree Press.

Reeves, D., & Reeves, B. (2016). *The myth of the muse: Supporting virtues that inspire creativity.* Solution Tree Press.

Reynolds, G. (2017, February 1). How to do the shortest workout possible. *The New York Times.* https://www.nytimes.com/2017/02/01/well/move/how-to-do-the-shortest-workout-possible.html?searchResultPosition=2

Roberts, W. (1990). *Leadership secrets of Attila the Hun.* Grand Central Publishing.

Rogelberg, S. G. (2019). *The surprising science of meetings: How you can lead your team to peak performance.* Oxford University Press.

Rose, D. M., Seidler, A., & Nubling, M. (2017). Associations of fatigue to work-related stress, mental and physical health in an employed community sample. *MC Psychiatry, 2017*(17). https://doi.org/10.1186/s12888-017-1237-y

Ross, F. (2018, June 8). *Stress vs. anxiety—knowing the difference is critical to your health.* Mental Health First Aid. https://www.mentalhealthfirstaid.org/external/2018/06/stress-vs-anxiety/

Ryan, L. (2015, August 23). The embarrassing truth about employee morale. *Forbes.* https://www.forbes.com/sites/lizryan/2015/08/23/

the-embarrassing-truth-about-employee-mo-
rale/#f82bf0257737

SafeStart. (2020, February 11). *A comprehensive guide to overcom-
ing the effects of fatigue in the workplace.* https://safestart.com/
news/a-comprehensive-guide-to-overcoming-the-effects-
of-fatigue-in-the-workplace/

Saleh, M. (2020, April 9). *A double whammy: The COVID-19
pandemic and burnout in medical professionals.* Harvard Medical
School. https://leanforward.hms.harvard.edu/2020/04/09/a-
double-whammy-the-covid-19-pandemic-and-burnout-in-
medical-professionals/

Sanner, B., & Bunderson, J. S. (2018, Winter). The truth about
hierarchy. *Sloan Management Review.* https://sloanreview.mit.
edu/article/the-truth-about-hierarchy/

Schaefer, J. (2019, April 10). *The root causes of low employee morale.*
American Management Association. https://www.amanet.
org/articles/the-root-causes-of-low-employee-morale/

Schorr, A., Carter, C., & Ladiges, W. (2017). The potential use
of physical resilience to predict healthy aging. *Pathobiology of
Aging & Age-Related Diseases, 8*(1). https://doi.org/10.1080/20
010001.2017.1403844

Schott Foundation. (2019, June). *Unacceptable: Nineteen states
still allow corporal punishment.* http://schottfoundation.org/
blog/2019/06/11/unacceptable-nineteen-states-still-al-
low-corporal-punishment

Schwartz, T., & Pines, A. (2020, March 23). Coping
with fatigue, fear, and panic during a crisis.
Harvard Business Review. https://hbr.org/2020/03/
coping-with-fatigue-fear-and-panic-during-a-crisis

Scott, K. (2017). *Radical candor: Be a kick-ass boss without losing
your humanity.* St. Martin's Press.

Senge, P. M. (2006). *The fifth discipline: The art and practice of the learning organization.* Crown Publishing Group.

Sherfinski, D. (2018, May 21). Students safer in school than out despite shootings, statistics show. *The Washington Times.* https://www.washingtontimes.com/news/2018/may/21/students-safer-school-out-despite-shootings-statis/

Shermer, M. (2005, September 5). Rumsfeld's wisdom: Where the known meets the unknown is where science begins. *Scientific American.* https://www.scientificamerican.com/article/rumsfelds-wisdom/

Shook, E. (2020, January 20). *Seeking responsible leadership.* Accenture. https://www.accenture.com/us-en/insights/consulting/responsible-leadership

Simmons, A. (2018, April 7). *Why students cheat—and what to do about it.* Edutopia. https://www.edutopia.org/article/why-students-cheat-and-what-do-about-it

Snow, S. (2020, April 23). *The counterintuitive thing about trust that explains why so many teams have issues with it.* LinkedIn. https://www.linkedin.com/pulse/counterintuitive-thing-trust-explains-why-so-many-teams-shane-snow/

Stephany, M. (2020). *How to understand the difference and similarities between anxiety and depression.* HealthPrep. https://healthprep.com/mental-health/how-to-understand-the-difference-and-similarities-between-anxiety-and-depression

Stevenson, H. (2020, May 15). *Authentic and responsible leadership.* Cleveland Consulting Group. http://www.clevelandconsultinggroup.com/articles/authentic-and-responsible-leadership.php

Summers, L. (2020, May 14). COVID-19 looks like a hinge in history. *Financial Times.* https://www.ft.com/content/de643ae8-9527-11ea-899a-f62a20d54625

FEARLESS SCHOOLS

Tierney, J., & Baumeister, R. (2019). *The power of bad: How the negativity effect rules us and how we can rule it.* Penguin Press.

Tynes, V. V. (n.d.). *Why punishment fails; what works better.* Premier Veterinary Behavior Counseling. http://www.nbvet-clinic.com/files/Why_Punishment_Fails_What_Works.pdf

Varol, O. (2020). *Think like a rocket scientist: Simple strategies you can use to make giant leaps in work and life.* PublicAffairs Books.

Walker, T. (2020, February 25). Unannounced active shooter drills scaring students without making them safer. *NEA Today.* http://neatoday.org/2020/02/25/active-shooter-drills-in-schools/

WebMD. (2017, February 17). *Depression recovery: An overview.* https://www.webmd.com/depression/recovery-overview

Wiseman, L. (2010). *Multipliers: How the best leaders make everyone smarter.* HarperBusiness.

Wolinsky, A., & Newfield, J. (2017, October 8). How to gain credibility when you have little experience. *Harvard Business Review.* https://hbr.org/2017/10/how-to-gain-credibility-when-you-have-little-experience

Zak, P. (2017). The neuroscience of trust. *Harvard Business Review, 95*(1), 84–90.

Zakrzewski, V. (2017, December 13). How to help students believe in themselves. *Greater Good Magazine.* https://greatergood.berkeley.edu/article/item/how_to_help_students_believe_in_themselves

INDEX

stress: versus anxiety, 77–78;
effects of, 72, 118; and fatigue,
66; recovery from, 73–77
structure: information on, 95;
and resilience, 62
substance abuse: and addiction,
60–61; and depression, 81
success, factors affecting, 126
Summers, Lawrence, 91
suspension, 101
sustainability: and exercise,
83; and leadership, 21; and
success, 126
swift trust, 17–18
systems thinking, 15, 142–54;
commitment to, 94; definition
of, 144–46; discussion
questions on, 153–54;
humility and, 150–51

talk therapy, 81
teachers: attrition of, 13, 29–30,
92; COVID-19 and, 73–74;
fearless, 110–12; rapid
feedback loops and, 149–50;
shortages of, anticipating,
91–92
10,000-hour rule, 64
therapy: for anxiety disorder, 79;
for depression, 81, 83
tough-on-crime stance, 49
trial and error, 108, 114
triggers, for depression, 82
trust, 1; building, 10–23;
destruction of, 39–55;
discussion questions on,
8–9, 22–23, 36–38, 55;
environment of, xv–xvi;

and fearless learning,
109; importance of, 3–9;
maintaining, 24–38; nature of,
11; neuroscience on, 10–12; in
peers, 113–14; in self, 114–15;
and success, 126; and systems
thinking, 143

unknowns, 93–96

values: and decision making,
100–102; unchanging, 119–
21, 147
violence, school versus home, 89

war room, term, 13
Whac-A-Mole, term, 142–43
working from home, and stress,
80
workplace, and exhaustion, 66
work stoppages, anticipating, 90
writing, 134–35
WYSIWYG, term, 26

yoga, and anxiety, 79